RADICAL SPIRITUALITY

RADICAL SPIRITUALITY

Repentance, Resistance, Revolution

JASON STORBAKKEN

Maryknoll, New York 10545

RADICAL SPIRITUALITY

Repentance, Resistance, Revolution

JASON STORBAKKEN

Founded in 1970, Orbis Books endeavors to publish works that enlighten the mind, nourish the spirit, and challenge the conscience. The publishing arm of the Maryknoll Fathers and Brothers, Orbis seeks to explore the global dimensions of the Christian faith and mission, to invite dialogue with diverse cultures and religious traditions, and to serve the cause of reconciliation and peace. The books published reflect the views of their authors and do not represent the official position of the Maryknoll Society. To learn more about Maryknoll and Orbis Books, please visit our website at http://www.maryknollsociety.org.

Published by Orbis Books, Maryknoll, New York 10545-0302.
Manufactured in the United States of America

Library of Congress Cataloging-in-Publication Data

Storbakken, Jason.
Radical spirituality : repentance, resistance, revolution / Jason Storbakken.
pages cm
Includes bibliographical references.
ISBN 978-1-62698-103-4 (pbk.)
1. Christian life. 2. Spirituality—Christianity. I. Title.
BV4501.3.S7627 2014
248—dc23

2014009004

To my wife Vonetta
and our children Chloe and Elgin

Contents

Acknowledgments

I cannot express enough gratitude to my mother Tammy Wolf (nee Storbakken) who, although never overtly religious, has consistently demonstrated the virtues of a life committed to genuine humility, radical forgiveness, dedication, and love. I am thankful to my father Mark Tschetter for his warmth, candor, and gift of storytelling. I am also grateful to my grandparents Ruth and, in memory, Elgin Tschetter (who passed away during the writing of this book) for bearing witness to Christ's love.

Many thanks to the Radical Living community, especially the founding members and their spouses (Melinda and Peter, Greg and Jolene, Alissa and David, and Molly), who have shared their lives with me and my wife for the last seven years. Many thanks also to friends of Radical Living, namely Becky and Kenny, but also the many others, who have walked alongside our community for many years. I am thankful to the Louisville Institute for providing me with a grant to formally begin this project; the Mennonite Church

USA, especially Warren Tyson, Sandra Perez, and Dave Greiser, who have consistently provided me wise counsel and spiritual strength; The Bowery Mission, particularly the community and ministry partners, but also the staff and students with whom I share most of my days; the Nurturing Communities Project, and David Janzen for his friendship and vision; and Orbis Books and my editor Jim Keane, for providing a grassroots theologian and practitioner a means by which to share his *radical spirituality*. I am also thankful for the friendship of New York City ministers and activists, particularly Alexie Torres-Fleming, Onleilove Alston, Rev. Dr. Gary V. Simpson, Rev. Conrad B. Tillard, Rev. Gwen Dingle, Rev. Dr. Peter Heltzel, Rev. Dr. Hal Taussig, James Macklin, James Winans, and George McCormack.

I am ever thankful for the love and support of my mother-in-law Corrine Blackmoore and my stepson, Kawansi Taylor, for bearing witness to his siblings the value of pursuing education and spiritual growth. I am thankful for the love of all my siblings and, of special note, Jacob Tschetter who I have lived with in various forms of community throughout my life.

And to my daughter and son, Chloe and Elgin, you fill my life with pure joy and great meaning.

Finally, and most importantly, I would like to thank my wife Vonetta. Your support, wisdom, and grace have allowed me the opportunity to mature as a husband, father, friend, and human being. Thank you for the light and love, truth and beauty that you shine into this world.

Introduction

Toward a Radical Spirituality

A genuine man goes to the roots. To be a radical is no more than that: to go to the roots.

—José Martí

This book is aimed at followers of Jesus Christ who seek a deeper, more authentic spirituality. It is aimed at those who have made mistakes on their spiritual journey and will undoubtedly take risks and make more mistakes as they pursue God. This is the story of my pursuit of God and the cloud of witnesses who have shaped me. I have had many failings in my life, and expect more struggles before this life is over, yet through these obstacles I have encountered a God who provides redemption and liberation, light and love to all who humbly, earnestly call upon the Holy Name. While this book is my personal story, that is, my testimony of Christ's work in my life, it is also a description of the theology and praxis that I have encountered as a disciple on the margins of the church as well as the margins of society.

My spiritual formation has been flush with contrast. My patrilineal, Anabaptist ancestry reaches deep into the seventeenth century. I grew up listening to my grandfather, Elgin Tobias Tschetter, tell the stories of our distant Hutterite and Mennonite kin who were hanged, burned, and stoned as martyrs of the faith. Yet I was born to an unwed teenage mother, far removed from the church, and too often I served as witness to the brutal ways she was emotionally and physically abused by boyfriends, exploited by employers, and limited by society's structures. As I came to faith in Christ, I sought to reconcile my personal experiences and my view of a church disconnected from those who truly need her with the teachings of Jesus Christ and the writings of the Holy Scriptures. It is for that reason that I have been drawn toward a radical spirituality. "Radical" merely means "from the root."

And, according to Paul's first letter to the church in Corinth, to be spiritual is to *try all things, examine, investigate, inquire into, question, and discern all things* (1 Cor. 2:15).[1] For the Christian, to move *toward* a radical spirituality is to start by returning to the rich soil in which we have been planted. It is to consider the seed sown and the roots that serve to hold us fast in the holy faith. We must examine our religious heritage and traditions, grow in knowledge of the saints who have walked before us, read and reread

---

[1] The *Amplified® Bible*, Copyright © 1954, 1958, 1962, 1964, 1965, 1987 by The Lockman Foundation. Used by permission. All rights reserved.

the prophets, psalms, Gospels, and other holy writings, and reflect upon our own Christian experience and perspective. It is as important to reflect on the experiences that birthed, shaped, and formed the primitive church as it is to understand the experiences that give meaning to our own personal spiritual life.

To be radical is to examine, with the mind of Christ, what we have been taught, to sincerely reflect on why we believe what we do, to continually return to the root teachings that anchor our faith, and to ask whether or not we truly practice what we proclaim to be true and right and good.

Radical Living

I should perhaps start with a personal admission: As a young man I lived deeply and intensely and often skirted danger in foreign countries. At age nineteen, seeking excitement and purpose, I trekked through the politically divisive Himalayan mountain state of Jammu and Kashmir in north India. At age twenty-two, I had been backpacking throughout South America for several months when my backpack—containing my journal, several rolls of film, and a little bit of cash—was stolen. In despair, I hitchhiked from Lima, Peru, to the city of Cartagena on the Caribbean coast of Colombia. There I laundered money for Mafiosi and lived in a brothel with Angolans in exile until I saved enough money to return to the United States. At the age of twenty-six, while teaching English in South Korea, I was charged with trafficking narcotics (but convicted only of usage), sentenced to several months in prison, and deported to the United States. I believe these experiences shaped and formed my worldview and theological imagination in many ways.

Upon my deportation, I returned to my hometown of Madison, Wisconsin, with a pile of debt, no job, and no money. I stayed with friends and family, trying to figure out the next step. After a month in Madison, I moved to Brooklyn, New York, to stay with a friend, crashing on his couch and looking for work.

It was in Brooklyn that I met the woman who would become my wife and co-laborer. In fact, she rented me my first room in Brooklyn. I waited for her on the stoop of the brownstone house that she was renting out. When I first saw her I knew that I had never seen such a beautiful woman in all my life, in all my travels. Her physical beauty was surpassed only by her grace, intellect, and compassion. We gradually formed a relationship and eventually moved in together. She continued to pursue investment real estate opportunities, and I attempted to establish myself as a writer in New York. I had written in the past for a variety of magazines and newspapers, and so had a portfolio of writing samples. I quickly landed work as a freelance writer and editor at magazines ranging from *High Times* to *Forbes*.

We were not always Christians. Vonetta emigrated with her family as an eleven-year-old girl from Guyana, the only English-speaking country in South America, to Brooklyn. Apart from college on Long Island and a brief stint in Texas, she has lived most of her life in Bedford-Stuyvesant, which has consistently been ranked as one of the poorest and most violent neighborhoods in New York City. Yet because she has always had the eyes to see the beauty of her neighborhood she has remained firmly rooted in this community. Vonetta witnessed firsthand urban decay—and renewal—as well as the devastating effects of the crack epidemic. Despite many obstacles, she graduated from college, earned her master's degree, worked in the nonprofit sector for several years, and in her late twenties she purchased a multifamily brownstone home.

When Vonetta and I met, we were both in the midst of personal struggles. She was dealing with family issues, while I was mentally, emotionally, and spiritually exhausted from serving time in South Korea. One morning on my commute into Manhattan to meet with an editor, a preacher boarded the A train and proceeded to proclaim the Gospel. I unsuccessfully attempted to ignore him. He spoke about how the church is not a Sunday morning destination. He said that God does not want to inhabit a building but wants to inhabit a people. It was not the routine fire-and-brimstone message of many subway preachers. It was peculiar. His message reawoke me to deeper things, and I gradually began to consider things of a spiritual nature. At the age of nineteen, I did come to faith in Christ and was baptized while in India, but my religion did not last long upon my return to the United States. The subway preacher awoke me to the encounter with God I previously experienced in India.

When I returned to the apartment I shared with Vonetta I told her about my encounter on the subway. I explained that somehow my faith had returned to me. Initially, she thought that I was breaking up with her. I moved out of the apartment we were sharing and rented a room in the neighborhood. During that time Vonetta too began to awaken to deeper spiritual things. We began to attend Sunday morning church services and midweek prayer meetings together, and eventually she came to faith and was baptized. We married within a year of our religious awakening.

Together we were ardently seeking Christ's headship over our lives. We regularly attended church services, and yet we still longed to be an active participant in the living, breathing body of Jesus Christ (i.e., the church). The subway preacher's message about the true church began to bear fruit in our lives. We came to the realization that instead of making church a weekly destination we would, as directed by the Scriptures (1 Cor. 12:12–27), seek to be participants in this living, breathing body. Thus, in August 2007, a few months after we were married, we opened our home to other followers of Jesus. The brownstone house became the flagship house of Radical Living, the Christian cohousing community my wife and I founded.

Vonetta christened the community Radical Living. As noted earlier, *radical* is a word that means "relating to the root." The term "radical" also gives homage to the Radical Reformation, particularly since my paternal ancestors were Hutterites, the most communal of all Anabaptists. We sought a return to primitive Christianity in an effort to move forward in our faith. We hoped to share our lives with others in a spirit of love and service. Almost as soon as we launched the faith community, our brownstone home was filled with Christ followers, and soon thereafter other houses on the block began to convert to community houses. Today the faith community consists of more than twenty people living within a one-block radius.

In essence, Radical Living is dedicated to a life centered in Christ, engaged in our neighborhood, and led by the Holy Spirit. My wife and I are an interracial couple—she is Afro-Guyanese and I am Euro-American—and thus we desire to maintain a diverse membership in the community.

We attempt to be a multicultural, intergenerational, and ecumenical community (Rev. 5:9) that seeks to embody Jesus' presence, particularly in our neighborhood. It is our hope that we will be a reconciled community—reconciled to God and to one another, regardless of racial, economic, or other perceived divisions.

Repentance, Resistance, Revolution

Vonetta and I founded Radical Living a few months after we were married. I left my work at *High Times*, a monthly magazine dedicated to marijuana culture, and other publications that I felt did a disservice to my faith walk. I landed a job at *Forbes* magazine in the editorial department, but after a year, just as earlier the Spirit had convinced me that my work at *High Times* was a hindrance to my Christian witness, so too did the Spirit convince me that my work at *Forbes*, although embraced by the dominant society, was a serious threat to my walk, particularly as it glorified wealth and encouraged mammon (i.e., the desire for material wealth and greed). I felt the Spirit moving me to work with the poorest of the poor. It was almost as if the Spirit were speaking audibly to my heart. I quit my work at *Forbes* and found employment as the staff writer at a think tank called the Institute for Children and Poverty. Shortly before our daughter, Chloe Zipporah, was born, I was offered my first position in ministry as the development director at Youth Ministries for Peace and Justice (YMPJ). I served at YMPJ for a few years and departed shortly after my second child, Elgin Melchizidek, was born.

I was privileged to serve in full-time ministry at YMPJ during the first few years of Radical Living. YMPJ, which is located in the poorest congressional district in the United States, was founded by Alexie Torres-Fleming in the mid-1990s and serves to equip young people with the skills to make social, economic, and environmental change in the South Bronx and beyond. It was at YMPJ, under the tutelage of Alexie (as well as Father Juan Carlos Ruiz, who was then the director of community organizing) that I began to develop a race and class analysis, and acquire a larger prophetic vocabulary with which to speak the language of resistance and revolution from a Christian perspective.

It was there that I began to understand more fully the systems and structures, powers and principalities that affect socially and economically disenfranchised communities in the South Bronx, Bedford-Stuyvesant, and those communities I had known as a child in the trailer parks and subsidized apartment complexes of southern Wisconsin. It was during those first few years at Radical Living, while also serving at YMPJ and meeting other like-minded people in New York City, who were also "seek[ing] first the Kingdom," that I began to recognize the themes of repentance, resistance, and revolution evident in marginalized communities.

Taking Action

One of Radical Living's first actions came about as the result of a series of Bible studies on the topic of immigration. After studying the Scriptures, we felt called to do more than simply share our lives together and learn about important issues. We desired to share with others the good news that we had learned: God dearly cares about the stranger, sojourner, and immigrant. We organized a symposium, called "Theology of Immigration: God, Immigrants and Activism," and invited local faith leaders from various organizations, such as Father Juan Carlos Ruiz who (apart from his work at YMPJ) had also cofounded the New Sanctuary Movement, Rev. Gabriel Salguero of the National Latino Evangelical Coalition, and Naomi Madsen of Justice For Our Neighbors, to share a message. A perk of living in New York City is that local faith leaders often have national recognition.

The symposium included a panel discussion with faith leaders and organizers, and the event raised financial support for several immigrant families who have a head of household caught in the deportation process. We also were able to organize a large, diverse group of people to participate in a weekly prayer vigil that continued for more than a year at the Varick Street Detention Center in lower Manhattan. I was encouraged to see people stretched and strengthened in their understanding of an issue vitally important to our city, and I was inspired to see people discover tangible ways to love their neighbors.

It is important that we as Christians practice what we preach. Therefore, praxis must accompany theology. Leading up to the season of Lent in 2011, I called faith leaders from around the city to join me for a visioning session at the headquarters of The Bowery Mission, where I had recently begun working (I currently provide pastoral care to the homeless community as the Director of Chapel and Compassionate Care). I had a vision for the city and wanted to invite other faith leaders to help me broaden and deepen that vision. As a result of that visioning session, we launched LentNYC: Lament, Repent and Re-imagine. For each week of Lent, churches, intentional communities, and small groups (and at least one convent of nuns) had a study guide with which they learned about an issue specific to the city, such as human trafficking, through a biblical lens and a social justice framework. During the week, each group was connected to an opportunity to volunteer or participate in a form of activism to directly engage with the issue. Prayer and fasting were also components of LentNYC. Participants were called to lament over personal sins but also the sins of the city, repent of wrong action or inaction, and actively reimagine (i.e., build) a new city of peace, justice, and love. Thousands of people throughout the five boroughs participated.

It is actions like Theology of Immigration and LentNYC, as well as daily activities like opening one's home to the homeless and sharing life in community, that are the result of attempting to follow Jesus. Because we continue to fall short of Christ's righteousness, we must take a continual posture of repentance, and as we turn from our self-centered, sinful nature, we turn toward a Christ-centered, holy nature of love and grace. As we follow Christ, we not only grow in a personal desire and ability to love others, we also begin to subvert the current system of oppression and domination, and thus make a way for God's Kingdom of peace and justice to enter in.

First and Foremost, Christ!

The Radical Living community was founded as an experiment to emphasize a Christian lifestyle and spirituality based around people sharing life together in a specific neighborhood. On a micro scale, we are attempting to shift the paradigm from an emphasis on the Sunday morning church service, which places prominence on professional clergy and a church building, toward a Christ-centered, community-based approach where the emphasis is on the people as a body indwelled by the Spirit.

This book began as a curriculum I developed for members of Radical Living. The curriculum consisted of exercises, conversation starters, and Bible studies on topics, such as sexuality and gender, exile and empire, and doctrine and dogma, that invited participants to engage with twenty-first-century urban issues through a Christ-centered, biblical lens. The curriculum was an attempt to digest some of what we had learned in community in the first several years and share that knowledge with others, particularly new members of Radical Living and others interested in returning to primitive Christianity. We were seeking a primal, or essential, Christianity and found Jesus' teachings and the model of the first-century church to be our primary example. This expands on much of the original material and introduces ideas not originally presented in the curriculum. It is also more personal and includes much of my own story.

First and foremost, although often unsuccessfully, I seek to find my identity with Christ, and where I find Christ is with those on the margins of society: the homeless, food insecure, prostitutes, and sick and shut in. As I attempt to live out my faith and articulate the reason why and how I follow Christ, I have become a grassroots theologian and practitioner. I make that statement as a declaration and as a disclaimer. This book is not necessarily about how to be a radical or how to be a *super*-spiritual person. Rather, this book is about my encounter and experience with God and the cloud of witnesses who continually shape me. It is about how I, my wife and children, and our faith community are attempting to move toward a radical spirituality. I hope that as you engage this book, you are challenged and encouraged to go deeper, to be rooted in Christ and radical in your spiritual journey, taking risks and allowing yourself to be tender and vulnerable so that you may be formed by God and the cloud of witnesses that surround you.

Chapter 1

When Did Discipleship Become So Casual?

Go therefore and make disciples.

—Jesus

Much of the church's history has consisted of casual discipleship and cultural Christianity. When the church's emphasis is not on Christ, but on the things of this world or things of a lesser spiritual nature, discipleship is marginalized. Some churches and even whole denominations find their primary identity, rather than in Christ, in the demonstration of spiritual gifts; or ritual, history, and tradition; or the reputation of a church or its pastor; or its political identity; or cultural relevancy; or any other such thing. These things have value, but when they usurp the primacy of Christ they undermine the very mission of the church, which, at her most basic level, is to make disciples of Jesus Christ. When

Christians compromise their faith by allowing it to be co-opted by politics or popular trends, their faith assumes the characteristics of the fallen world. Life in the Kingdom of God demands that we pursue holiness.

Discipleship is for the ardent and devout seeker of God who hopes to be more like Jesus in every area of his or her life. It is for the humble and teachable Christian sister and brother who recognize that to grow spiritually they must lean on others who have more wisdom, experience, and maturity. Discipleship is for those who are willing to be countercultural to society and the current trends that dominate the church. It has most often occurred on the margins of the church because it is radical and transformative; it affects the very core of the person and challenges the social and religious status quo.

Christ, the one upon whom we are to model our life, was crucified, as were many of the apostles (the disciples closest to him). This does not mean that we too must suffer bodily death. It does mean that we must be willing to make great personal sacrifices if we are to be like Christ. In a church that values discipleship, those whom the world considers weak are strengthened by others who support them; the poor are liberated from their oppression, and the rich are liberated from their privilege; emotional, spiritual, and material resources are shared because there is abundance in the Kingdom of God.

There is a tension in the institutional church where, on the one hand, she embraces parishioners who exhibit virtues of meekness and servanthood while, on the other hand, she resists those filled with the Spirit of Christ who prophesy against the vices of the institutional church (including hierarchical oppression and paternalism) and proclaim the Kingdom in solidarity with those whom society has cast off, but God has called. The church too often fosters a passive laity where parishioners attend Sunday service and accept as their ministry, for example, a role of usher or greeter on Sunday morning rather than embracing their true ministerial calling to carry forth Christ's mission *in the world.* The church has created a culture of Christianity that neglects spiritual formation and accepts cultural Christianity to the detriment of her mission to make disciples.

Cultural Christians do not embrace discipleship because the institutional church has placed other labels on them: laity, parishioners, or congregants. Seldom are they called disciples. The casual Christian does not attend church to be transformed or to be better equipped to help usher in God's Holy Kingdom. Many casual Christians, akin to cultural Christians, may have grown up in the church, or perhaps they are married with children and want to impart to their children the importance of a tradition and a value system, or they attend Sunday services simply to be inspired.

For the last half century, variant streams have existed within the Western church that have served to divert the faithful from the mission of the church. Two of these dominant streams include (1) an overemphasis on cultural relevancy (often in the guise of church planting) and (2) the polarizing effect of bipartisan politics.

Cultural Relevancy

Jesus did not say, "Go and plant churches." Neither did he say, "Go and devise strategies for church growth." The Great Commission is to make disciples, yet a major emphasis in Western Christianity is church planting. The focus has shifted from the original desire of Jesus, and the body of Christ is suffering for it. The tension rests on whether followers of Jesus Christ should plant churches as a means to make disciples or focus on making disciples where the fruit of discipleship is the formation of churches (i.e., local bodies of believers).

Church planters take courses and seminars that address target financial goals, ethnic and economic demographics of the church they want to grow, and best methods to attract new members (most of whom are not new converts to Christ but members of other churches who are looking for a new experience). Many church planters invest their time and resources to attract and entertain, rather than transform and equip those whom they are serving. They invest in buildings, professional staff, and technology more readily than they invest into the lives of the poor and marginalized, community development projects, and the spiritual formation of those they serve.

Many who attend church expect to be entertained via music, lighting, an inspirational speaker, and other such things. In turn, church administrators expect to meet the bottom line of a church's operating budget in order to provide the desired experience of the membership. Planting a church is a labor-intensive endeavor that entails budgets, building or leasing a space to gather, hiring professional clergy and administrators, purchasing audio/visual equipment (including microphones, musical instruments, projectors, and computers), and much more. Making disciples in a relational way requires less in the way of financial and organizational resources, yet requires greater personal sacrifice to invest in the spiritual formation of the less spiritually mature sister or brother.

Today, many evangelicals, Anabaptists, and mainline Christians travel to attend churches that reflect their cultural identities (ethnic, economic, political, and more), although in Catholicism this trend occurs far less than it used to. Until the 1960s, Catholics often attended ethnic parishes, so that there might be three Catholic churches on the same street—an Irish, an Italian, and a Polish church. There has been an attempt to shift toward a parish, neighborhood-centered model by several denominations and churches, yet many people are still willing to travel great distances to worship with others who look and think as they do, to have their biases reinforced. Because the church invests more in the Sunday morning *show*, so too the people put on a show. They wear their Sunday best and put on their best face, but this is not church. If a person endures personal suffering, he or she is often hesitant to share that pain because we do not want to appear different (poorer, weaker, less educated) from others.

As the pastor of the homeless community at The Bowery Mission in Manhattan, I meet a broad range of people. One young man, I'll call him Mike, I have come to know quite well; in some ways he exemplifies the failings of the institutional church. Mike is in his late twenties, has two master's degrees, and grew up in a Christian home. He is a member of a wealthy and well-known church in uptown Manhattan where he serves as an usher and is active in a small group. Mike lost his job and became homeless. He was without housing for nearly a year. He received many of his meals at the Mission and participated in the clothing and shower program twice a week. Mike told me that during his time of homelessness, he grieved alone. He still attended church and his small group, but none of them knew what he was experiencing. He was not willing or able to be vulnerable with those whom he should have been able to trust and lean on as his sisters and brothers.

Rather than place the burden on Mike (such as arguing that he should have taken the risk to share his struggle with those whom he fellowships) or the institutional church (such as arguing that the church has created a system that does not allow for relationships of deep trust and vulnerability), it would be better to find a way to restore the church to a place of health and vitality. When the church values discipleship, we recognize that all of us are students on the journey with Jesus. We have much to learn, there will be mistakes, and none of us have it all together. We must be willing to go deeper with one another, trusting each other so that we may strengthen and encourage one another in the faith.

We must not confine the church to the space within four walls. We must examine how we "do church." Most churches, whether Pentecostal or Episcopalian or otherwise, meet weekly on Sunday and sometimes midweek for a prayer meeting or small group. People check in for two hours, sing some worship songs, listen to an inspirational message, and then check out until next Sunday. It is not that the average churchgoer leaves church and enters into gross sin, but that he or she remains in the shallow waters of faith, and community bonds are not deeply formed. People have been entertained and uplifted, but not transformed and equipped.

Cultural relevancy serves to attract people to church, but there comes a point when church must transcend attractionalism to become transformative. There comes a point when the church must become the living, breathing body of Christ. The beauty and truth of the simple Gospel, in word, but particularly in practice, is attractive and relevant for all who humbly and sincerely yearn for the peace, hope, and healing in Christ's announcement of the coming Kingdom.

Politicization of the Church

A second dominant stream that diverts the faithful from their mission is the politicization of the church. The church has been co-opted by the American Dream. She is wed to politics and too often resonates more with the popular culture than with God's Holy Kingdom. The dominant narrative espouses a self-centered, individualistic ethos focused on superficial happiness and the acquisition of political power, rather than a Christ-centered emphasis on holiness, mature piety, and sacrificial love.

There have always been court priests and court prophets who endorse systemic structures even when those structures oppress and exploit whole segments of society. In America's two-party system, these court priests and prophets continue to exist on both sides. The liberal-conservative paradigm is a false construct that serves to separate people into ideological camps. And these priests and false prophets help to perpetuate that division for personal gain.

In the United States, the prophetic church of the Civil Rights Movement has been usurped by the Religious Right, and less effectively by the Religious Left. The prophetic has been replaced by the politic. The church is (mis)aligned to political parties and policies that seldom affect real change. As Christians, we must not veer left or right, but center on Christ and deepen in the Word. Like the prophets, we must be willing to speak truth to power while also speaking the truth *with* those whom the powers perceive as powerless.

American Christians too often find their identity in their reaction to two hot-button political issues: abortion and gay marriage. For some, this is the litmus test as to whether one is a true Christian. Many arguments against both abortion and gay marriage claim some sort of adherence to "natural law," which is not necessarily dependent on Scripture; similarly, many arguments on behalf of gay marriage and prochoice stances, even among Christian groups, focus more on rights than on God's inclusive love; for example, the rhetoric of prochoice Christian groups seems to focus more on each woman's dignity than on God's love. Unfortunately, these important issues are often weighted with rhetoric that perpetuates culture wars rather than provides opportunities for real dialogue and possible creative responses to address these vital issues.

Several years ago, I had the opportunity to witness a season of discipleship between two women who brought to the surface the nuances of abortion. Let us call them Irene and Jean. Irene is an older, fairly conservative Christian woman, and Jean is a young woman new in the faith. Irene invited Jean into her home when the young woman was in a time of crisis. During that time, it was revealed that Jean was pregnant. Irene was prolife, and encouraged Jean to keep the child, and even offered either to raise the child along with Jean or raise the child herself until Jean was in a better position to care for the child. After much consideration,

Jean ultimately decided to have an abortion. Irene had made it clear what she believed but still accompanied Jean to the clinic.

Irene did not pressure Jean or try to manipulate her in any way, but she did hope she would change her mind even as she sat in the clinic. Jean went forward with the abortion. Irene expressed no judgment and even provided spiritual and emotional aftercare for Jean. Irene cared for the souls of both the unborn child and the mother. Irene and Jean were both deeply grieved by the abortion, but Irene provided much needed support and wisdom.

Jean felt some relief after her decision but also a great deal of guilt. Irene continued to minister God's grace, mercy, and love to Jean, and continually reminded her that she is dearly loved by a Holy Father. Irene went beyond political rhetoric. She extended herself for the sake of the mother and unborn child. She left judgment to God and demonstrated God's abundant love to this young woman. If only the church would demonstrate this kind of love and sacrifice, rather than empty rhetoric and strong opinions. Always, in the midst of a weakening and decaying church, there remain vestiges, perhaps best expressed as a remnant of saints dedicated to following the Way of Jesus. Irene, and others like her, remain this vestige of hope for many lost due to their circumstances.

Another diversionary issue for Christians is the role (or nonrole) of sexual minorities in the church. Depending on one's sources and norms, there are a variety of places one could go with this issue. I value the Bible, and read clearly in the Hebrew Scriptures as well as the New Testament the Levitical decree and Pauline proclamation that state that certain forms of homosexuality are sinful. Yet, I contend that all life apart from God is sinful, in that *sin* means *separation from God*. Biblical literalists argue that the Bible explicitly states several times that homosexuality is an abomination and thus should not be condoned. Although Jesus uses heteronormative language, he never mentions homosexuality, and sexual orientation is never considered a sin in the Bible. It is also valuable on issues like this to turn to the stories of the Scripture, narratives that describe a situation contrary to decrees and moral teachings. One such story is that of the Ethiopian eunuch.

The first non-Jewish convert to the Christian faith was a sexual minority. The Ethiopian eunuch who met Philip while reading an Isaian text, a text that he did not understand, possibly did not have testicles and thus would not have been allowed into the Jerusalem temple. And, as it goes with eunuchs, he may have found himself in compromising sexual situations (e.g., some eunuchs were used as sexual mates for male and female nobles). But now a man (possibly with no testicles and whose sexual orientation is questionable) is rejoicing in the Lord! (Acts 8). Christ, and his good news, meets us where we are; he opens us to new possibilities; and through his Word we can find hope and a deep sense of purpose for our life, regardless of what society or other religious types might say.

Furthermore, the idea that the sin of Sodom was homosexuality, another biblical example often used to condemn homosexuals, is misplaced. Sodom was an urban center known for vice. Angels visited Abraham and told him that they were on their way to destroy Sodom because its sin was so grave. Abraham attempted to convince the angels not to destroy Sodom. He asked, "Suppose there are fifty righteous within the city; will you then sweep away the place and not forgive it for the fifty righteous who are in it?" The Lord replied that he would not destroy the city if there were just ten righteous people. The sin of Sodom, according to the Bible, is not homosexual relations. Ezekiel writes, "This was the guilt of your sister Sodom: she and her daughters had pride, excess of food, and prosperous ease, but did not aid the poor and needy" (Ezek. 16:49).

If we as Christians are to uphold every word in the Bible as applicable for our cultural context, then we must not pick and choose. For example, Jesus says that we are not to divorce, yet Christians divorce as frequently as non-Christians and no one bats an eye. Paul's first letter to the Corinthians, which many quote to uphold homosexuality as a sin, also explains the faithlessness of those supposed Christians who take others to court; it continues that thieves, the greedy, and gossips will not inherit the Kingdom of God. Yes, that group of people who attend church every Sunday and sing the hymns the loudest, yet talk about everybody else at their weekly luncheon! They are in the same category as men having sex with men. The Scriptures also state that we must not call people *fool* or *idiot*, or else, according to Jesus, we are in danger of hellfire. That is biblical literalism.

Shifting the Paradigm

We must shift the paradigm. We must no longer let the loudest voices lead. We must return to a model of church that has a focus on spiritual formation of the individual as well as the collective. The American church today is similar to ancient Rome in its focus on the physical building and professional clergy. Yet this is not how it has always been, particularly in times of spiritual awakening. First-century Christians regularly met in homes. From the fourth through sixth centuries, as a reaction to the institutionalization of the church, many of the devout departed urban settings for the deserts of Palestine and Egypt—they went to the margins of empire into the wilderness to connect with God. Some Christian movements over the centuries, such as the Hutterites, never had church buildings until modern times. They recognized that the church is the body of believers and that where two or three are gathered in Christ's name, there is the church. We must shift the paradigm of the notion of church as the place where people gather to an understanding of church as the people whom God inhabits.

Since my wife and I founded Radical Living, our focus has been twofold: (1) to provide opportunities for the spiritual formation of those who live with us in community and (2) to build relationships in our neighborhood. Since 2007, I have organized and facilitated seasonal gatherings of New York City's intentional communities (Bruderhof, Franciscans, new monastics, Catholic Workers, and others) to share skills, foster intercommunity relationships, and strengthen the movement. Vonetta and I did not start the community with the intent to fill the void of discipleship in the church, yet we have found that it does serve that purpose, at least on a micro level. Many members of Radical Living have become leaders in their local congregations, which raises the question, "Does the intentional community attract deep Christians, or does it serve to equip average Christians with a deeper sense of calling?"

In Matthew 4:23–5:2, the crowds followed Jesus because they were sick and demon-possessed. The crowds gathered around Jesus to be healed, to be delivered from demonic possession, to witness miracles. Scripture says that Jesus went up the mountainside and sat down, and the disciples came to him to receive a teaching. There is a distinction between the crowds and the disciples. Jesus healed people so that they might simply live, so that they might be restored to family and society. The lepers, epileptics, and demon-possessed sought him out for healing and restoration. They were outcasts, and Jesus brought them back into community. The disciples went further. They sought Jesus not merely to witness his miracles of healing and exorcism, but also to receive his teaching, to learn how to live, and ultimately to usher in a way of life that will bring healing and restoration to the world. We need to choose whether we are merely in the crowd following Jesus from a distance, getting from him what we need, or if we are disciples following him, walking close to him, and learning from him how to live, celebrate, and suffer.

Chapter 2

Jesus the Radical

Prior to my conversion, I was the roving reggae reporter for *High Times* magazine from 2004 to 2006. I was well acquainted with the festival and concert circuit, and had intimate access to the scene. After my conversion, I still found myself backstage at concerts, but rather than smoking fat spliffs and interviewing reggae artists like Sean Paul or Buju Banton for an article, I was engaging Rastafarians and reggae artists in conversations on a wide range of spiritual topics. These conversations eventually developed into Conquering Lion Ministries, a grassroots evangelistic outreach to the Rastafarian community in New York City.

I was new in my faith and fairly zealous. Although I have always had an aversion to tract evangelism—personally, it seems patronizing and I am skeptical of its effectiveness—I felt compelled to create a tract. On the front it asked, "What did Haile Selassie say about Jesus Christ?" Haile Selassie was the Emperor of Ethiopia during much of the twentieth century. Before assuming the imperial throne, his name was Ras ("Prince") Tafari Makonnen; hence adherents are called Rastafarians. When he was crowned emperor he chose the name Haile Selassie ("Power of the Trinity") to represent his Christian tradition. Despite his confession of faith and commitment to Jesus Christ, many of those who call themselves Rastafarians worship Selassie as Christ, the second coming, or another form of God incarnate.

My initial intent with Conquering Lion Ministries was to reach the Rasta community with the Gospel message and show that Selassie was not God but that he himself confessed Christ as Lord. Yet the more time I spent among devout Rastas, and not (as they say) baldhead Rastas (those who wear dreads as fashion, but do not adhere to the strict dietary or moral codes), the more I began to respect deeply the Rastafarian sense of counterculture and exile identity. The American church has seldom had that sense of otherness toward the empire (or as the Rastas call it, Babylon). I learned that there are three main branches, or houses, of Rastafari: Bobo Ashanti, Nyabinghi, and Twelve Tribes. Of these houses, Twelve Tribes is closest to orthodox Christianity. They confess Christ as Lord and see Selassie as having been a divinely appointed king in the Davidic dynasty. They do not use the name Jesus because it was used by enslavers and colonialists. Instead they use the original name of Yeshua HaMashiyach. "Yeshua" is "Jesus" and "HaMashiyach" is "Messiah" in the Hebrew language. To most Rastas, the anglicized name of Jesus is but one tool in the white supremacist's arsenal of domination and oppression.

Many Rastas understand firsthand, due to a history of slavery and colonization, how Christianity has too often been co-opted to colonize minds and oppress whole groups. More than once upon looking at the religious tract, a Rasta turned to me and asked, "Who do you think Jesus is?"

The question of Jesus' identity has been around since Jesus first asked his disciples, "Who do people say the Son of Man is?" People are still wrestling with this question today. Was Jesus a moral teacher, philosopher, insurrectionist, prophet, savior, Son of God, or something altogether different? His disciples answered Jesus' question by listing the names of several prophets—Jeremiah, Elijah, John the Baptizer, and others. Then Jesus turned the question to his disciples: "But who do you say that I am?" Peter, always ambitious, steps up: "You are the Messiah, Son of the living God." Jesus' response is affirming; he promises to Peter the building of the church and even promises Peter the keys to the Kingdom. He blesses Peter and tells him that this knowledge was revealed to him "by my Father in heaven." A few verses later, the joyous affirmation turns somber. Jesus explains to his disciples that he must go to Jerusalem where he will be persecuted and even killed by the religious and political elites, but on the third day he will be raised. Peter, dwelling on Christ's death rather than the hope of a resurrected life, objects and says, "God forbid it, Lord! This must never happen to you." Jesus turns and says to Peter, "Get behind me, Satan! You are a stumbling block to me; for you are setting your mind not on divine things but on human things" (Matt. 16:23).

Too often we place expectations on God that are formed by our own desires. The first-century Jews expected Christ to appear as a warrior king. The Jews had been dominated by foreign powers for many centuries, often displaced and forced into exile, overtaxed, and occasionally conscripted into wars. They yearned for the Christ who would liberate them from their oppressors and restore Israel to her former glory. When, at last, Jesus was revealed to be the Messiah, his disciples were confused and disheartened. How could their Savior, the Messiah, who is the Son of God and creator of the heavens and earth, allow himself to be killed?

Because so many were expecting a warrior king, they were disillusioned that Jesus would allow himself to be taken into custody and suffer crucifixion. That is perhaps one reason why the crowd before Pontius Pilate clamored for Barabbas to be released rather than Jesus. Barabbas was an insurrectionist, charged with sedition. Scholars purport that Barabbas was in prison because he attempted a violent overthrow of the Roman occupation of Israel. *Bar* means son, and *abba* means god (or rather it is a term of endearment for god, akin to "papa"); thus Barabbas[1] means "son of god." Jesus the Christ or Barabbas the Insurrectionist? We must ask ourselves which son of God we want to live in our lives and in our world, the one who forcefully takes what he believes to be rightfully his, or the one who heeds his Father's will even in the midst of suffering and persecution.

After Christ had been crucified and laid in the tomb, no one suspecting that he would conquer death, he appeared to his disciples. In at least one instance, Jesus breathed on his disciples and they received the Holy Spirit. In that subtle act of intimacy, their faith was bolstered, and they began to understand the profound significance of the life, death, and resurrection of Jesus Christ as prophesied through the writings of the Hebrew Scriptures. The disciples had followed

[1] http://www.biblestudytools.com/dictionary/barabbas/.

Jesus throughout the course of his ministry, but seldom did any suspect that Jesus was the Christ, and those who did suspect did not understand that this Christ would manifest himself in ways counter to the messianic expectations of the first-century Judean populace. The breath, the very Spirit of the Risen Christ, awakened them to the reality of the countercultural expression of the Kingdom of God, and its radical implications for this world.

In a similar fashion, Christ in his sublime yet dramatic nature entered into my own world. I had heard the Nativity story my entire life, but it was not until I first read the Scriptures for myself that I experienced God's embrace and desire to redeem my own nativity story. Like Jesus, I was born to an unwed, teenage mom on the margins of society. My mom and I lived below the poverty line most of my childhood. We moved often and lived in low-income apartments, a trailer, and the occasional duplex, and we were homeless on more than one occasion. By most accounts, Mary was around fourteen or fifteen years old when she conceived Jesus. She was betrothed, but not yet married, and she was from Galilee—a region of Israel occupied by, and hostile to, the Roman Empire. Both births were scandalous, but unlike Mary (who conceived Jesus by the Holy Spirit) my sixteen-year-old mom conceived me with a fifteen-year-old neighbor boy named Mark.

In recognizing the ways in which God chose to descend into this world and even condescend to a humiliating situation—he spent his first night sleeping in a trough and his last hours nailed to a tree—I am comforted by the Almighty God. We can know that he empathizes with our circumstances and cares for even the most outcast and seemingly defeated people in society. In addition to the nativity and the crucifixion, there were other parts of Jesus' story that resonated deeply within me and other parts that challenged me to break through into a new reality.

When Mary learned that she was pregnant, the angel Gabriel comforted her and bolstered her faith that the promised Messiah would soon arrive—and she would be his mother! The Israelites, and particularly the Galileans, were an economically and socially oppressed people eagerly awaiting the arrival of the Messiah to usher in the Kingdom of God. The promise of the birth of the Messiah brought hope to a people on the margins of society.

Galilee was heavily taxed by Rome, which kept the local population, including, presumably, Mary's family, in deep poverty and debt. Historians have documented many Galilean uprisings and grassroots insurrections against the Roman occupation of Israel, specifically against the heavy taxation of the region, immediately preceding and during Jesus' formative years. Jesus surely grew up hearing these stories of uprisings. This social unrest and desire for justice is evidenced by the song Mary sang during her pregnancy. While visiting her elderly cousin Elizabeth, who was miraculously pregnant with Christ's forerunner, John the Baptizer, the Holy Spirit fell upon them and they began to rejoice in the hope of the Lord. During this visit, Mary sang the song recorded in Luke 1:46–55.

> My soul magnifies the Lord,
> and my spirit rejoices in God my Savior,
> for he has looked with favor on the lowliness of his servant.

Surely, from now on all generations will call me blessed;
for the Mighty One has done great things for me,
and holy is his name.
His mercy is for those who fear him
from generation to generation.
He has shown strength with his arm;
he has scattered the proud in the thoughts of their hearts.
He has brought down the powerful from their thrones,
and lifted up the lowly;
he has filled the hungry with good things,
and sent the rich away empty.
He has helped his servant Israel,
in remembrance of his mercy,
according to the promise he made to our ancestors,
to Abraham and to his descendants forever.

Did you catch the revolutionary sentiments in this poor, pregnant, unwed teenage girl's song? She yearns for the restoration of the material and spiritual loss of her people, and she expresses urgency for wrongs to be made right. *He has brought down the powerful from their thrones and lifted up the lowly; he has filled the hungry with good things, and sent the rich away empty.* Who are the rich, and where are they being sent away to? It is my suspicion that it is the Romans, and those local religious and government leaders who conspired with them, who are *rich* because they tax the Galileans' food production, which in turn keeps the local population poor and hungry. When the Romans (the high and mighty) are *sent away*, there will be enough food to fill the hungry with good things.

This passage refers to a very specific cultural context, but it also applies to our own times. Who are the high and mighty today? They may not wear tunics and live in Rome, but they are still the ones who oppress, exploit, and do injustice to the poor, the fatherless (single mothers and their children), sexual minorities, the stranger (immigrants), and the disabled. They are those who put their trust in politicians and political systems, in themselves and their own personal happiness, rather than in Christ, his cross, and the coming Kingdom.

In Jesus' adulthood, in the fullness of his ministry, he echoed his mother's song when he said,

> But woe to you who are rich,
> for you have received your consolation.
> Woe to you who are full now,
> for you will be hungry.
> Woe to you who are laughing now,
> for you will mourn and weep.
> Woe to you when all speak well of you, for that is what their ancestors did to the false prophets. (Luke 6:24–26).

Returning to Mary, pregnant with God, we see that she deeply and dearly understood the messianic aspirations of an oppressed people. Soon after she gave birth, the family was displaced by Herod's infanticide. It is intriguing to think that the Magis' gift of gold may have helped fund the family's trip to Egypt.

Eventually the holy family returned to the village of Nazareth in the region of Galilee where Jesus was raised.

Jesus' life between the ages of twelve and thirty years old is called the *eighteen years of silence.* There are no stories about what he did during this time. The last mention of his childhood is a story of when he was twelve years old and absconded from his parents during a visit to Jerusalem, visiting the temple courts and sitting among the teachers, listening to them, asking questions, and even providing his own insight and answers. The final word on Jesus' childhood says that "And Jesus increased in wisdom and in years, and in divine and human favor." These eighteen years of silence would better be called the eighteen years of preparation.

Jesus again appears on the scene at the age of thirty when he is baptized by his cousin John in the River Jordan. He soon returns to his hometown to begin his ministry. As Jesus entered the synagogue the same Spirit that descended upon him at his baptism and soon thereafter drove him into the wilderness now filled him with the overflowing fullness of God. It is here that Jesus proclaims his mission and the purpose of his ministry. He begins by reading from the Isaiah scroll.

> The spirit of the Lord God is upon me,
> because the Lord has anointed me;
> he has sent me to bring good news to the oppressed,
> to bind up the brokenhearted,
> to proclaim liberty to the captives,
> and release to the prisoners;
> to proclaim the year of the Lord's favor. (Isaiah 61:1–2a)

This passage is rooted in the Hebrew idea of jubilee found in Leviticus 25:8–53. Jubilee is a biblical regulation that restores homes to the homeless, sets slaves free, and cancels all debts. It is interesting to note that when Jesus read from the Isaiah scroll he skipped verse 2b, which mentions the "the day of vengeance of our God." When Jesus is talking about the poor, blind, imprisoned, and oppressed, he could easily be talking about the disenfranchised of our society: the chronically homeless, drug addicts and alcoholics, the incarcerated, undocumented immigrants, and veterans damaged by war and discarded by their governments. It is to them that he is proclaiming "the year of the Lord's favor." It is to them he is proclaiming hope! Christ has come, his Kingdom is entering in, and the gates of hell will not prevail.

After reading from the Isaiah scroll, Jesus sits back down and proclaims "Today this scripture has been fulfilled in your hearing." The people in the pews listening to Jesus responded well—at first. The Scriptures say they "spoke well of him and were amazed." They understood themselves to be poor, overtaxed, oppressed, and occupied by a foreign power. But then Jesus lays on them words they do not want to hear. Yes, the Savior has come and he has come for all—whether Jew or Gentile, Roman or Greek; today, Jesus' words might mean American or Libyan, North Korean or South Korean, Republican or Democrat, rich or poor—Jesus has come to save all.

He tells the synagogue congregation how in the days of the prophets Elijah and Elisha, there were many widows and lepers in Israel and a great famine was over the land. Like today, there were people who felt alone, abandoned, sick, and hungry. But the prophets went to those outside the covenant—they went beyond Israel because Israel, like the church today, was sick with idolatry (erecting gods to militarism, nationalism, and other isms and schisms). The prophets did not go to the widows and lepers in Israel; Elijah went to a widow in the pagan region of Zarephath; he multiplied her food and raised her son from the dead. Elisha healed Naaman's leprosy although he was a Syrian, not only from a foreign nation, but from an empire hostile to Israel.

We are called to Zarephath and Syria. We are called to be present to the outcast and marginalized. We are called to bring healing and hope even to those outside the covenant, to those outside the church walls. We are called to love those who are considered unredeemable. And it is Jesus who is calling us.

Jesus did not despise the brokenhearted; nor did he cast out the outcasts. He did use strong language with the religious hypocrites—calling them snakes, murderers, and vipers. The exclusionary religionists, such as the synagogue congregants in Nazareth (or many modern-day fundamentalists), assume they have a monopoly on access to God and act as if it is up to them to determine who should (or should not) receive grace and restoration. The Pharisees were indignant when Jesus told them that the tax collectors and prostitutes will enter the Kingdom of God ahead of them. Today, exclusionary religionists, whether liberal or conservative, would be up in arms if one were to claim that those who broker subprime mortgage loans and those who identify as transgender will enter the Kingdom of God ahead of them.

He did not equate himself with David the king, but David the brigand. In Luke 6, after Jesus and his disciples pluck and eat grain on the Sabbath, he is questioned by the religious elites. Jesus compares himself to David who, along with his men, ate the shewbread in the temple, which was not lawful for any but priests to eat. During this time, David was a wanted man, pursued by the authorities. Jesus compares himself to the outcast and outlawed David, a man pursued and persecuted. Over and over again, Jesus finds identity with those on society's margins. If we are looking for Christ in the midst of power, it is likely that we will miss him.

Who do you say I am? It is my personal conviction that during Jesus' ministry, he was an exorcist, healer, and wandering charismatic. He was not homeless in the Western sense of the word; he was an itinerant teacher and rabbi. He was persecuted by certain religious Jewish leaders for claiming to be equal with God, and he was convicted as a criminal on charges that he posed a threat to the occupying powers (i.e., he was considered to be a king in opposition to Caesar). Summarily, he suffered a state-sponsored execution in the form of crucifixion. On the third day, his physical life was resurrected. In that final act, he conquered death and sin. He is the savior of humanity and creation. He is prophet, priest and king, son of the living God, and second person of the Holy Trinity.

Chapter 3

Church as Revolutionary Movement

Those who are one with Christ in Spirit, love, and life, who teach that which was commanded by them by Christ, namely, repentance and the peaceable Gospel of grace . . . are the body and bride of Christ, the ark, the mount and garden of the Lord, the house, people, city, temple of God, the spiritual Eve, flesh of Christ's flesh and bone of his bone.

—Menno Simons

My paternal lineage can be traced back to sixteenth-century religious radicals called Hutterites. Although I did not grow up in a Christian home and infrequently went to church as a child, my spiritual formation began at a tender age, and much of it had to do with Elgin Tschetter, my paternal grandfather, telling me stories of our Hutterite and Mennonite forebears. Throughout my childhood, my grandparents demonstrated the love of Christ with their life. My grandma ministered for more than twenty years to incarcerated women in the jails of southern Wisconsin and took many mission trips to India. Yet my grandfather is the one who had the greatest influence on my early spiritual formation.

My grandfather always claimed that his spiritual gift was to be a bold and faithful witness to the Gospel. Throughout my life, he has not only shared the Gospel with me, but also pointed to the evidence of God's presence all around us. When I was a child, we often sat in the backyard and stargazed, sometimes with a telescope, and occasionally he would wax almost poetic about the creator God in a way that inspired within me a desire to participate in a holy creation. He took me to church as often as I was willing to go, and after Sunday lunch he regularly talked about the sufferings our Anabaptist ancestors endured for the faith. Although he stood in opposition to the pacifism of the Anabaptists and adamantly opposed the communalism of the Hutterites, he was proud of our religious heritage. Through stories, my grandfather connected me to our ancestral heritage and imparted to me the importance of faith in Christ.

Although not raised in a Hutterite colony, I have been formed and inspired deeply by the stories passed down to me. The Hutterites arose as a movement within the Radical Reformation. They are absolute pacifists; practice believer's baptism, which is the practice of one's baptism following their profession of faith; and for most of their history, they have lived communally. It was my grandfather's stories of their total commitment to the way of Jesus that shaped my understanding of what it means to be a follower of Jesus. My grandpa was raised near the Hutterite colonies in South

Dakota, and he can trace his ancestry to early leaders in the movement. Our family line, the Tschetters (I have my mother's maiden name), have been Prairieleut (noncommunal Hutterites) for many generations. Among all Anabaptists, which also consist of Amish and Mennonites, the Hutterites are the most communitarian.

The Hutterites were persecuted by both Catholic and Protestant churches, and some were even taken as galley slaves on Ottoman Empire ships. During the Middle Ages, one's baptism into a church was akin to one's allegiance to the state. When the Hutterites confessed believer's baptism as the true way to express one's allegiance to the Kingdom of God, proponents of the Holy Roman Empire as well as Protestant church-states throughout Europe deemed them subversive because they renounced their earthly citizenship, refused to participate in wartime activities or pay military taxes, and chose to live collectively. These proponents ordered Hutterites to be beheaded, burned at the stake, and driven from their homes in an effort to crush their movement.

The Hutterite lifestyle is based in large part on the biblical Book of Acts and the practices of the primitive church. The Hutterites share meals in a large dining hall, own very few personal possessions, and give their whole life to this other way of living. During the height of persecution of the Hutterites in Europe, a lord of an estate who was sympathetic to the Hutterites gave them a parcel of land and offered them protection. But when the tyrants (ordered by Protestant religious leaders, such as Zwingli, or Protestant monarchs, such as the Tudors, or Roman Catholic authorities, such as Ferdinand I, who served as

Holy Roman Emperor) arrived to kill the Hutterites, they would not allow the lord of the estate's men to defend them. They would not allow others to shed blood on their behalf. Instead, like sheep led to the slaughter, they went to the tyrants and were martyred in droves. And yet it was during these times of persecution that the Hutterite community grew. This is similar to the first few centuries of the church when, it is said, that the blood of the martyrs served as seeds for the church.

The Hutterites became a seminomadic Christian community and spent considerable time in Eastern Europe and spent nearly a century in southern Russia before moving to the United States in the 1870s. They decided to leave during the Russification of the late nineteenth century, when Russian communities were being forced to abandon their language and their culture, young men were drafted into the military, and religious freedom was severely threatened. Two men, Paul and Lorenz Tschetter, were designated to scout the United States in the hope that it would allow them to practice their religion freely. Paul (who was my grandfather's great-uncle) was the Servant of the Word, which is a Hutterisch term for minister and leader, and Lorenz was his uncle. After visiting with Mennonites and traveling across the United States, the two men met President Ulysses Grant, who explained to them that he could make no commitment there would be no war, but that he was confident that the United States would not engage in a major war for at least fifty years, and thus they would be free from the threat of military service. This was more than the Russian government was able to offer the Hutterites, and so they migrated to the Dakota Territory.

True to President Grant's word, there was no major war for fifty years, but soon thereafter WWI broke out and young Hutterite men began to receive draft cards. The men who were drafted refused to participate in wartime activities and were sent to prison. Some went to Alcatraz and were then transferred to Leavenworth. Several of these men were tortured and killed by government officials while in prison. They were martyred for their faith and commitment to peace and loving one's enemies.

My first direct paternal ancestor in the United States was Paul's younger brother, John. Whereas Paul provided pastoral (and practical) leadership to the five thousand Hutterites as they migrated from Russia to the United States, John was prophetic and visionary, experiencing ecstatic revelations. In the cellar of his home, John sought God in prayer. He claimed that a light washed over him, and it was then that he was spiritually born (i.e., born again). He had a born-again experience but did not have the language to articulate it, since the "new birth" is not part of Hutterite theology. He met with Pentecostals decades before the Azusa Street Revival, which occurred in 1906 and ushered in the current movement of Pentecostalism. John appreciated the Pentecostal emphasis on healing, the gifts of the Spirit, and end-times prophecy, but he struggled with their level of emotional intensity. He soon met Rev. Jacob A. Wiebe (for whom my great-grandfather is named) and was baptized in the Wolf Creek in rural South Dakota, which was then the Dakota Territory. It was winter and the men had to cut a hole in the ice at Wolf Creek to baptize John.

Wiebe was a Russian Mennonite who was dissatisfied with the state of the Mennonite church in the late nineteenth century. He called for greater piety and deeper devotion to Christ and his teachings. After an unsuccessful attempt to reform the Russian Mennonite church, Wiebe founded the Mennonite Brethren denomination. John Tschetter was one of his early disciples, and served as a zealous revivalist and preacher. John began to make disciples. They gathered in homes, and when the faith community grew, they moved their meeting to a barn and eventually built a church. When the church grew too large, they spawned new churches for people to gather. The goal was not to increase the membership of the church, but to make disciples.

John evangelized many of the Prairieleut and communal Hutterites, traveling to many states and even into Canada to share his experience of spiritual birth and personal relationship with Jesus. John is noted for bringing about spiritual revival and renewal across the Dakota Plains and elsewhere. Because John had such a significant impact on the spiritual life of so many, and is considered the father of many churches, he was called Johann Feta, a Hutterisch moniker translated as "Father John." Although he passed away in the mid-twentieth century, he is still referred to by many as Johann Feta. Apart from farming, he served as founding pastor of several churches, including Bethel Mennonite Brethren Church, located near Huron, South Dakota, and Salem Mennonite Brethren Church, which celebrated its 125th anniversary in 2011, and is located near the Tschetter family's original homestead. John's wife Susana, his parents, and much of his family were eventually born again. Although his elder brother Paul remained Hutterite, many of Paul's children had a born-again experience and joined the Mennonite Brethren.

In fact, Father John ordained and commissioned Mennonite Brethren missionaries, one of whom was Paul Tschetter's son, to serve in Boone, North Carolina, and plant integrated churches of whites and recently freed blacks. They also founded several orphanages and schools. They were truly radical about Christ's love and the building up of the Kingdom of God. Today, after many years of opposition, including Ku Klux Klan rallies on their lawn and death threats against the ministers, six of those churches continue to thrive.

In the fall of 2012, my wife and I and our two young children visited the region in South Dakota where my Hutterite ancestors settled in this country in the early 1870s, hoping to gain a deeper connection to our spiritual forebears and to *remember* those who came before us. We were able to visit the places that I had mostly only heard of. As I researched my ancestors, communalism, and models of discipleship, I discovered a deep connection to my grandfather's grandfather, Rev. John Tschetter. We visited the first homestead and saw the cellar where John, as a man in his early twenties, had a vision of God's light wash over him. We also visited Wolf Creek, where John was baptized, and spent time on Hutterite colonies with distant kin. We visited churches that John founded and were inspired that the last church, Bethel Mennonite Brethren, where he ministered for more than forty years, is still doing great work in their community and throughout the world. Bethel Mennonite Brethren has missionaries on almost every continent, and the Sunday morning we visited, the message delivered by Pastor Coalt Robinson explored the personal and social impacts of revolution rooted in the Gospel. The membership of the church continues to value an intelligent and informed faith, compassionate expression of that faith, and commitment to share Jesus' good news.

It is important to visit and revisit stories and places to recognize the myriad ways that the Kingdom of God enters into this world, through individuals, families, communities, and movements. We do not need to live under tyranny and the threat of persecution to be faithful disciples of Christ. Yet it is important to remember the price paid by Christ and by all the witnesses who have suffered for the faith over the last two thousand years. These martyrs, these witnesses, point to the truth of the Gospel message. The blood of the Lamb reminds us of the cost of Christ's conviction and moves us from a place of complacency to a place of devotion and active participation in the body of Christ.

Too often, as Christians, we forget those who came before us who lived sacrificially, who were true witnesses to a living faith. When we forget their stories, we become weak and numb and distracted. We suffer due to our forgetfulness and lack of mindfulness. It is often said that the church thrives in places where she is persecuted. It is in these places of pain and persecution where she most intimately remembers the Gospel story, and it is in these places where we are most inspired to live out even the most challenging of Jesus' teachings.

Seeking the Other

It was these stories of perseverance in the midst of persecution, heavenly visions, and love for the oppressed and even their enemies that gave early shape to my faith. Although my Grandpa Tschetter grew up in the Mennonite Brethren Church, under the pastoral care of his grandfather, Johann Feta, he left his Anabaptist tradition as a young man and became a Fundamentalist Baptist. Unlike his Mennonite parents, he was never a pacifist and struggled with the basic tenets of the Anabaptist expression of faith. The Baptists were more in line with his religious reasoning. As a teenager, I found myself inspired by his stories of our Hutterite ancestry but at odds with my grandparents' fundamentalism. Around the age of fifteen, I had a crisis of faith. I occasionally went to church with my grandparents but was no longer convinced by the claims of the Christian faith, or at least not how I understood them.

The hurt and brokenness I suffered as a child without the stability of permanent housing, witnessing men abuse my mother, and wondering why the church seemed so impotent, set me on my pursuit of "otherness" at a young age, whether that otherness be God or a mystical experience or anything other than the reality I had been dealt. Despite my rejection of the Christian faith that was handed to me, my soul longed for spiritual wholeness. I sought to experience the intimacy of losing myself in infinity. I hoped for visions and was open to the fantastic, and longed to encounter the Other. I began to practice meditation, which I initially learned by watching Kung Fu movies as a preteen in the 1980s. I asked my aunt, who was on furlough from the mission field in India (she and her husband have served the deaf in India since the late 1970s), what she thought about meditation. She said, "It all depends what you are meditating on." Until that point I merely practiced the cessation of thought. I meditated on nothingness and simply sought clarity of mind, which is much more difficult than one might assume.

In my early teens, I was often in trouble with the authorities. I was a shoplifter, vandal, fighter, drinker, and drug user, and whenever the police picked me up for my outlaw behavior, I was ordered to do community service because I was a juvenile. The courts ordered me to clean city vehicles, or pick up litter in parks, but most often they ordered me to work in the public library. It was in the library that I discovered spiritual and subversive texts that gave voice to my angst and frustration. I began to read books on various types of yoga, and I especially enjoyed reading the scriptures of Eastern religions. The first Eastern script I read was the *Dhammapada*, a Buddhist text I stumbled across while doing court-ordered community service at the library.

It was during this time of intensely pursuing the Other that I began regularly to smoke marijuana, experiment with other drugs, and engage in sexual activity. In my reading of countercultural and subversive works, I identified with anarchists and nonconformists. Henry David Thoreau's essay on civil disobedience spoke deeply to my soul. I did not want to submit to any worldly government. "Let my conscience be my government" was my plea. Whitman's *Leaves of Grass* was my bible. I carried it everywhere and memorized stanzas and whole poems. I did not want to live in a world of prose but sought to dwell in poetry, creativity, and ecstatic revelation. The devotional poems of Rumi and other Sufis inspired me toward divine intoxication. I began to fast and abstain from various worldly pursuits for various lengths of time as a spiritual discipline. The purpose of religion and spirituality began to take a new shape in my life. I read the early church fathers and Eastern mystics side by side.

At the time, I listened to Bob Marley and The Doors almost religiously. Bob Marley's message of love and justice spoke to my hope for redeeming the broken parts of my life, and the Dionysian frenzy of Jim Morrison and The Doors supported my youthful desire to experience great golden copulations of mythic proportions. I reveled in Rimbaud and to a lesser extent Baudelaire, and read the great American litany of Beat writers. William Seward Burroughs' desire to break the mold of the human race stirred me to deep conviction, as I too sought to break the mold into which I had been cast. I plotted adventures and looked forward to when I would be freed from the confines of the small town and small world in which I lived. I desired to experience vast expanses of earth and heaven, mind and soul.

Throughout my teen years, I hoped that visions would awaken sensibilities within me to create alternate realities of my own. I spent mornings and afternoons chanting *Om* and other strange mantras I discovered in books. I committed to memory and often recited the Tibetan prayer, "*Om mani padme hum*," which means "there is a jewel in the lotus," but I was especially fond of the ornate Hindu mantras such as "*Om namo bhagavate vasudevaya*." I experimented with breathing techniques, especially pranayama but also hesychasm. Pranayama is a breathing technique developed within Hinduism, whereas hesychasm is a breathing technique developed within the Russian Orthodox Church. Both breathing exercises are meant to provide a way toward transcendence.

Upon discovering the works of Swami Vivekananda, I gave myself over to the pursuit of psychic development and the liberation of the soul. I began to experiment with Kundalini yoga and the practice of projecting astral visions. I sat in the lotus position, eyes fixed on infinity, gazing into the middle of space, and considered deep-sky objects, subatomic particles, and universes that existed before me, within me, and within each breath. I inhaled through my left nostril, chanting and concentrating on the breath traveling down the left side of my spinal column to strike and awaken the serpent coiled near my tailbone. I then exhaled from my right nostril, chanting and concentrating on the breath carrying the serpent that traveled up the right side of my spinal column to strike my mind's eye, and awaken hidden visions and secret intellectual prowess.

Having read that Beat poet Allen Ginsberg achieved mystical revelations while reading William Blake's *Ah! Sunflower*, I, a youth in the rural country sticks of Wisconsin, broke out in search of that vision. I committed to mind and heart each verse, word, syllable, sound, and sensation of Blake's poem. I inhaled whole consonants and exhaled vowels. I consumed the word. Other works and personalities revealed themselves to me on my pursuit. Dionysian incarnations, eastern avatars, and desert priests in ancient Persia intoxicated by the divine were contemplated and summoned. I engaged the word and responded with poetry.

I practiced imagining and reimagining the vision set before me. I deconstructed mountains and clouds, space and matter, rearranged particles, redefined terms, invented words, and developed new sentence structures. By dismantling systems, I hoped to erect and resurrect new structures and systems that offered hope and promise rather than the intellectual and spiritual oppression I had encountered in public schools, church, and society. I hoped dull, desensitized persons (such as Thoreau's "mass of men who lead lives of quiet desperation") would awaken to the fullness of life and that dead systems and decaying structures would be cast aside so that new structures could be established.

I was convinced that old systems and depraved mentalities needed to be destroyed. Radicals and prophets, saints and holy insurgents needed to arise to subvert the system by any means necessary to make way for the new reality. And while my mind marveled at the hope of another way, I was still unable to fathom the mystery of *what* or *who* would usher in this revolution. What I did know was that this new way was all around me; I could almost touch it, and yet I struggled to enter fully in.

Two weeks after graduating high school at the age of seventeen, I left home to seek visions. I spent the next ten years traveling across North and South America, Europe, Africa, and Asia, working a variety of jobs ranging from grill chef in barbecue joints to track maintainer for a regional railroad company to freelance writer; I studied for a couple of years at a community college and transferred to the University of Wisconsin. Along the way I participated in spiritual communities and social experiments. I lived with anarcho-primitivists in the American Southwest, Hare Krishna groups in Europe, Christian missionaries in India, and squatters in London, and as an undergraduate I participated in the cooperative movement in Madison, Wisconsin.

Hare Krishna

At the age of nineteen, I bought a one-way ticket to London. I had saved enough money from a factory job to purchase the ticket and allow me some pocket money but not much else. I knew I needed a plan. The day after I arrived, I met two Hare Krishna devotees selling books in Trafalgar Square. They were not much older than me. I asked where they were staying, and they pointed me to the Soho temple. That evening, after much waiting, I was given a bed.

In exchange for room and board, I participated in their rhythm of study, worship, and work. I read voraciously the classic texts of Vaishnava Hinduism, which is the branch that worships Vishnu (and his many incarnations) as the ultimate deity. I was particularly attracted to the stories of Chaitanya, the sixteenth-century Hindu saint who was a major proponent of Bhakti (or devotional) yoga. Chaitanya is considered by his adherents as the full incarnation of Krishna, yet—and this is where it gets very creative—he is in the mood of Radharani, Krishna's consort (and lover). Radharani, despite being married to another man, was completely devoted and in love with Krishna. She could not resist his flute playing and, along with other maidens, often joined Krishna for rasa-lila, the dance of ecstasy.

I later found certain parallels between the theological undergirding pertaining to Chaitanya and God's self-revelation in Christ. For example, as Krishna in the mood of Radharani is modeling for his disciples how to live a devout life, so too it is Christ, who is the fullness of God in human form, who models for his disciples how to live a holy life.

God as revealed in the Hebrew and Christian Scriptures is often referred to as a groom and/or a lover. And Israel (as well as the church) is referred to as the bride and beloved. For example, in the Revelation Christ is the groom, and the church is the bride. In Hosea, the prophet is told to marry Gomer, a prostitute, as a means of representing God's relationship with Israel (who chases after foreign gods). Perhaps most closely related to the Bhakti yoga perspective is Song of Songs, which is often interpreted as the relationship between God and Israel (or, from a Christian perspective, Christ and the church). It is of note that the lover and beloved in Song are unmarried (there is no marriage contract or ketuba, and they have to sneak around) just as Radha and Krishna are not married to one another.

What are the implications of God in erotic relationship with the collective of his worshipers? And, even if we interpret this relationship as prudent and chaste (which is a stretch when we examine the Scriptures), what does it mean when the groom and bride do ultimately consummate their wedding vows. As RadhaKrishna are often engaged in a dance of ecstasy, is the ChristChurch also called to such profound intimacy and eroticism? Where are the followers of Christ who seek him with their whole being, who suffer when they are not near him, who long for their Lord's closeness? Might stories and theologies from other traditions serve to awaken the Christian imagination that God desires a deep, intimate relationship with his beloved?

In many ways, my time with the Hare Krishna stirred my theological imagination. I met spiritual teachers and visited the estate John Lennon donated to the International Society for Krishna Consciousness (ISKCON), the formal name of the Hare Krishna Movement. Radhanatha was the first genuine teacher of Hinduism that I met. He was one of the first disciples of Prabhupada, the founder of ISKCON, and is revered as one of the most influential leaders of Gaudiya Vaishnava Hinduism in the world. He was visiting the London temple for Janmashtami, Krishna's birthday celebration. Many devotees fawned over him, but because I had no concept of who he was, I was rather skeptical. One afternoon he gave a talk to a large group explaining how everyone in the room must have lived good past lives to be now a human. During the question and answer portion, I raised my hand and asked how he knew that a fly does not have the same sense of self-importance that each of us had. Perhaps it was my teen angst or spirit of seeming defiance, but Radhanatha appeared at first flustered and taken aback. After the meeting, we met again and became friends. He invited me to join him at John Lennon's estate for the Janmashtami celebration. Upon his departure from London, he gave me the contact information for his temple in Bombay, which was the first place I visited when I eventually arrived in India several months later. During the next six months as I traveled across Europe, I stayed in Hare Krishna temples, in abandoned buildings occupied by squatters, and with new friends I made along the way. After a brief stint at the temple in Paris, I eventually hitchhiked from Paris to Madrid.

Most of the devotees in Madrid left for India soon after I arrived, and the leader of the temple asked if I could stay to help. I agreed. The two devotees who remained included a devout and disciplined young man whose father was a high-ranking politician in Spain who had disavowed his son for becoming a Hare Krishna devotee. The other young man had been a devotee for more than five years but recently had developed doubts and was in the process of moving out. The first week after the group departed for India, we spent time figuring out roles, sharing meals, and cleaning the temple. By the second week, two musically inclined Swedish brothers joined us, and we began singing Hare Krishna mantras over Nirvana music played on the harmonium and kartals in the plazas on the weekends. Our weekend chants led many young people to visit the temple during the week. We started serving free lunches in the temple, and very quickly we were filled to capacity every noon. Young people began to join, and we even created a special women's dormitory.

We remained disciplined and woke up each morning at 4:30 a.m. to pray and meditate. We took turns teaching from texts such as *Srimad Bhagavatam,* and we held regular bhajjans, devotional music services. Word spread that a revival was happening at the Madrid temple, and we were visited by leaders of the organization. During my time in Madrid, I discovered truths about religious community such as the importance of discipline, study, enthusiasm, and group participation. When the devotees returned from India, I decided that it was my turn to visit the subcontinent.

Entering the Church

My grandparents helped me to purchase a one-way ticket to Bombay. Their investment would prove to be well spent. I flew from Madrid (with one layover in Kuwait) to Bombay (this was before its name was changed to Mumbai). It was 1997—the Hale-Bopp Comet was in the sky and India was celebrating its fiftieth year of independence. I was nineteen years old and still yearning for a genuine connection to God. I had made friends among the Hare Krishna and gleaned certain spiritual truths up to that point, but I had yet to encounter the Living God. I spent a few days at Swami Radhanatha's temple in Bombay before traveling to my aunt and uncle's mission in Ootacamund, a hill station in the Nilgiri Hills of Tamil Nadu. During that time they had a school and church for the deaf. They allowed me plenty of space and did not press their religion on me. In fact, I had to ask my uncle for a Bible, which he gladly gave me.

I immersed myself in the Bible and spent much of my time talking about spiritual things with my uncle. I arrived in early December, spent the holidays with my missionary family, and then departed for the Himalayas; I spent a month there reading the Bible, smoking charas with devotees of Shiva, and visiting ancient Hindu temples. It was there that I began to leave the way of other religions and walk the way of Jesus.

When I returned to Ootacamund, I spent a day immersed in prayer and reading the Book of Isaiah. Waves of grace washed over me. I went from reading Isaiah to prostrating on the floor before God to resting in God's presence in meditation in the forest adjoining my aunt and uncle's house. I felt that Jesus, the fullness of God in human form, was for me. God's choice to enter into a situation of poverty and persecution made me feel like God entered into this world for me and to identify with the poor and outcast.

The truth of the Gospel shook me to my core, and it was then that I decided to give my life to the way of Jesus. Whereas earlier in my spiritual journey I was unable to fathom the mystery of *what* or *who* would bringing healing to the broken parts of my life and the world, I now understood that it is Christ and his way of peace and justice that ushers in this new way of living and healing together. Through Jesus I was able to enter into the very presence of God, the Holy of Holies, and be shaped and formed and filled to overflowing by God's love, truth, and beauty. I felt forgiven, and I felt that I had the power to forgive those who caused me harm. I wanted to be baptized. Easter was near, so I heeded my uncle's advice to wait until Easter Sunday to be baptized.

I used the following weeks to prepare for my baptism. I prayed, read the Bible, and spent ample time talking with my uncle. On Easter Sunday, there were several of the older students from the deaf school also getting baptized. The water tank for my aunt and uncle's home doubled as the baptismal font. My uncle's co-pastor, Daniel Mani, opened the tank and found a dead mouse floating on top. He threw it out and asked with a sly grin, "Ready to get washed clean of your sins?" All the students gathered for the service. My uncle delivered a message, and then we proceeded to the baptismal font. I entered in. It was waist-deep. My uncle asked me a few questions pertaining to my confession of faith, and then I was fully immersed into the water. I emerged from the water feeling new, cleaned, and made whole. I was ready to follow Jesus.

I was in India a total of six months and away from the United States for one year. Although it was in India that I believed in Jesus and his Word, it took me a long time to understand and submit to the way of Jesus. Upon my return to the United States, I regularly attended my grandparents' church—the same church that I occasionally attended as a child—but struggled to find people with whom I could connect. Like many churches that I have experienced, most people already had their minds made up regarding religious doctrines and political and social perspectives. I needed to wrestle with these ideas to make them truly my own. The church in North America seemed to be co-opted by nationalism and the dominant culture. I still retained my nonconformist and anarchistic convictions. The American flag waving in the church seemed an offense. Nor did I understand how a Christian could pledge allegiance to a flag or any ideology that was not centered in Christ. Eventually I stopped attending church altogether and returned to finding my main identity in the world rather than Christ.

Doing Time in South Korea

In May 2003, when I was twenty-six, I graduated with a B.A. in international studies from the University of Wisconsin-Madison. That summer, I returned for a fourth and final season to the regional railroad company where I had worked as a track maintainer. I drove spikes, set ties, and laid rail alongside seasoned and grizzled railroaders. In October 2003, during the slow season, I requested a voluntary layoff so I could collect unemployment and pursue work related to my degree.

Since I have an international studies degree, I decided to seek employment abroad. I arrived in Amsterdam and spent most of autumn as a houseguest of Dutch friends. I passed my time patronizing coffee shops and enjoying marijuana's legal status, journaling and writing poetry, and exploring the city's museums and canals. I intended to find residence in Warsaw, Prague, or another large Eastern European city and write freelance articles for English-language, expatriate newspapers in the former Soviet bloc. But, as will happen when traveling, my plans changed.

As winter approached, the idea of spending a harsh, snow-laden season in Eastern Europe was replaced by thoughts of sunny Morocco, a country with a rich culture, and one that allowed me to continue cultivating a connoisseur's taste for cannabis. I trekked vast expanses of the Atlas Mountains, spent several weeks mesmerized by the surreal nature of the sun-scorched Sahara, and rehydrated by lounging in Essaouira and other cities along the Atlantic and Mediterranean coasts. I applied for teaching positions in Casablanca and Marrakech, and looked for Moroccan-based, English-language publications, to no avail. When my unemployment benefits expired, I returned to the United States.

I was rapidly exhausting my savings account and desperately seeking a steady source of income when a friend told me that he was considering teaching in South Korea. He said there was ample opportunity, and the money was good. Korean ESL academies (called *hogwon* in Korea) even paid for round-trip airfare and housing. After researching ESL academies online, I applied for a teaching position through a recruiter in South Korea. After a series of interviews, I was on my way.

My closest friend in South Korea was my co-worker, Sam, a thirty-year-old Korean American from New York City. He was a confident character with a checkered past. He had studied at NYU as part of a prisoner-education program while serving time at Rikers Island. He had surrendered his U.S. citizenship when he came to Korea about five years earlier as part of a plea bargain to reduce his jail time in America. After a couple of days, Sam asked me, "Do you smoke?" He knew I didn't smoke cigarettes, so I understood he meant cannabis. "Yep," I confided. From that point on, Sam and I casually smoked together. Later, I learned that Sam was a dealer and actually made more money selling hashish than he did teaching English.

Three months into my one-year teaching contract, I was sent to a detention center for nearly three months, fined thousands of dollars, and eventually deported for smoking hashish. It was a harsh experience. Dark clouds hovered low and rain drizzled on the day in August 2004 when we were arrested. At the prosecutor's office in Seoul, we were fingerprinted and photographed. The investigator said we were facing federal criminal charges. Our arrest, it turned out, traced to a drug sale that Sam had made through the mail to a man named James. When James was arrested, he implicated Sam, who in turn gave up the names of people he had smoked with and sold to in an attempt to reduce his own sentence. I was convicted of usage because no drugs were found on my person or in my apartment. Sam was charged with possession and trafficking. We were then taken to Songdong Detention Center.

While serving my time, I read much of the Old Testament and was particularly struck by the story of Jephtah in the Book of Judges. Jephtah was the eldest son, his mother was considered a harlot, and he was deemed an outcast. He ran with bandits and adventurers (depending on the Bible translation) but eventually returned to deliver his people, the Israelites, from the Ammonites. Much tragedy befell Jephtah, but he was used by God. And so I figured that if God could use Jephthah, he might be able to still work through me. Jepthah's story resonated with me, and I slowly began my journey back to faith in God.

Upon my deportation, I eventually settled in Brooklyn, New York. It was in Brooklyn that I met Vonetta, the woman who would become my wife. Vonetta had moved from Guyana to the Bedford-Stuyvesant neighborhood of Brooklyn when she was eleven. At the age of sixteen she had her son, Kawansi, who is now a law student at the American University in DC. With support from her mother, Vonetta was able to study business and theater in college. Upon graduating, she worked five years as a case worker with adults who have multiple sclerosis. During that time she worked toward buying a house, and just before we met she purchased a multifamily brownstone. Vonetta occasionally went to church as a child, probably about as much as I did. She identified as Anglican, although that had no deep significance in her spiritual life. When we met, neither of us had any type of spiritual life to speak of. We lived together. She continued her work, and I found my niche as a freelance writer.

Subway Preacher

A couple of years into our relationship, I was on the A train traveling to meet with an editor when I heard a subway preacher proclaiming the good news. Normally, I would not pay attention to the ranting of what I perceived to be a religious fanatic, but he gave a peculiar message about the true church that began to awaken something deep within me. He explained there is one church, and she is the living, breathing body of Jesus Christ. The subway preacher proclaimed, "The church is not the building where Christians gather on Sunday; rather it is the Christians themselves who gather that makes the Church. The

Lord does not want to inhabit a building, but wants to inhabit a people! Christians are the living stones, cut and shaped and fit together, that create the temple of the living God." He talked about the false church that looms like a shadow over the true church, and how people have been deceived into believing that the false church is the place to find salvation. "The shadow looks powerful, but it is an illusion. The real Church is the community of brothers and sisters united in Christ serving one another, loving one another (and even their enemies), and discovering ways for the Kingdom of God to enter this world."

It was on the A train listening to this man preach about the true church where I felt the rush of the Holy Spirit wash over me. Others on the train continued about their routine—reading papers, listening to music, chatting—as I did most days. But at that moment, somewhere beneath the East River between the High Street and Delancey Street stops, I had a profound encounter with the Spirit of the Living God. The Spirit filled the entire train car, it filled all time and space, and weighed heavily upon my soul. The Spirit, I realized, had always been fully present. It was I who lacked presence to God. I could not resist turning to my God.

It was at that moment that I had my Pentecost experience. The Spirit of the Lord was upon me. I had confessed Christ and was baptized years earlier, but it was not until that moment that I felt the fullness, severity, and implications of a life at the crux of radical conversion. The Spirit took me to a place of deep consecration, and I felt an urgency to share my experience with any who would listen so that they too might awaken to the presence of the living God. But first I needed to find a way to articulate my experience and newfound freedom. I needed to change my lifestyle and give all to God.

When I returned to the apartment I shared with Vonetta and told her about my experience, she thought I was breaking up with her because I told her I was moving out and I was acting differently. Shortly after my subway conversion, Vonetta also began to experience spiritual transformation. Although her childhood in Guyana was influenced by British colonialism and thus Anglicanism, she did not find much identity in Christianity. Upon moving to New York she attended a Christian summer camp and occasionally went to church, but that was the whole of her Christian experience. My wife had purchased a house shortly before we met, and with the great blessing of becoming a homeowner, she also felt the stress and burden that often accompanies blessing. And so she began to seek refuge and strength in God.

I did not have any Christian friends in New York, so after talking together and doing an online search, Vonetta and I decided to visit a multicultural megachurch. We started by attending a Sunday service and quickly became regulars, rarely missing a Sunday service and attending most midweek prayer meetings. We eventually became members, joined the prayer band, and were active in the evangelism ministry, in which we walked across the Brooklyn Bridge handing out tracts. On occasion, I preached on the subway. My girlfriend was baptized in the church, and we were even married by one of the church's pastors. During our two years of active membership, we received many blessings and grew in faith.

Our time at the megachurch helped us to establish a spiritual foundation. We learned the importance of prayer,

Bible reading, and worship. After a couple of years, however, I hit a plateau in my spiritual growth. I began to feel restless during the service. Church had become a distraction—the building, stage, and lights—from my worship of God.

We began to raise questions: Why was it that one person, the pastor, did the bulk of the speaking? Why did all the people in the pews face the pastor rather than one another? Why did leaders in the church encourage a passive laity, rather than encourage others to develop their many gifts? Did not the Word say that every member of the church has a gift to contribute: a song, a poem, prophecy, a teaching, or word of encouragement? Why was there a distinction between congregation and clergy, when the Scriptures describe a priesthood of all believers?

The Spirit was moving my wife and me to another place. We began to seek God in prayer and search the Scriptures for answers. I recalled the subway preacher whose words first called me back to the church: the church is the people, not the building. It was the realization that God does not want to inhabit a building, but wants to inhabit a people, that led my wife and I to consider how we might be the church, how we might participate in the living, breathing body of Jesus, and how we might help usher in this Kingdom that Jesus says is present and yet breaking in.

We considered what skills, gifts, experiences, and resources we could give to the Kingdom. My wife has a business degree and experience in property management. My experience as a young adult in the cooperative movement was helpful. In 2007, two months after we were married, we opened our brownstone home in Brooklyn to other followers of Jesus. We advertised rooms-for-rent in church bulletins and on Christian websites. We grew quickly; within a year we had three community houses. Today there are a couple dozen members of Radical Living who live in several buildings within a one-block radius of one another.

Our multifamily home quickly filled with believers, and we began to meet for shared meals, Bible study, and prayer. My wife and I decided to visit New Orleans shortly after Katrina and considered planting a church there. When we returned to the little community forming in our home, we realized that God was already doing work in our lives and had given us a ministry. We were still active members of the megachurch. Although I continued to grow in discouragement by the structures of the institutional church, this was not a criticism of just our church, but the church in North America. My wife and I had formed very few deep relationships with other believers at the church and, although the church is charismatic, I felt that my spiritual gifts were stagnated by the hierarchy and institutionalism of the church. It was frustrating to worship God with thousands of other believers in such an individualistic way. We all faced the same direction, raised our hands in worship, closed our eyes to concentrate on God, and every service the pastor would ask the congregants to shake hands or hug the person next to them. My wife and I desired deeper relationship with our brothers and sisters in Christ, but even in the midst of thousands of worshipers, there was a disconnection with those around us.

Eventually we left the megachurch for a neighborhood church. Since we felt called to invest in our neighborhood, we decided it would be best to worship in a church where we could walk on Sunday morning. Gradually, Radical Living became our community of accountability and primary faith community.

Learning from Saints

As the Radical Living community grew, we began to study early church history and look for other communities and movements similar to what we were experiencing. The Book of Acts and letters of the New Testament gave us a view of life in the first church. We also read the Didache, and writings by Tertullian, Pachomius, and Antony. We learned that for the first three hundred years, the church gathered in homes, Christians met each other's needs, and they sought to be of one heart, one mind, and one accord (Acts 4:32–34).

We discovered that there was a major shift in church practice in the fourth century. In 312 CE, Constantine was the first Roman emperor to convert to Christianity. The church shifted from being a Spirit-led movement of the people to a state-funded and state-endorsed religion of empire. When Christ gave up his Spirit on the cross, the veil that separated the people from the Holy of Holies tore in half, allowing all people immediate and intimate access to God through Jesus Christ. When the church became co-opted by Constantine's religion of empire and domination, the veil was seemingly re-placed over the Holy of Holies.

For the first three centuries, there were Christians who served in the military, but all church leaders taught absolute peace. The church that proclaimed *Peace* became the church militant, placing crosses on shields before entering battle. Within a couple of decades of Constantine's conversion,

Augustine of Hippo coined the term "Just War," which was later developed into the Just War theory, the church's most prominent position on war. A hierarchy developed; bishops, deacons, and priests were approved (and often appointed) by magistrates in the Roman Empire.

Communion shifted from a festive, communal meal to a somber religious observance. With the conversion of Constantine and the co-opting of the church, only a priest was allowed to administer Communion, thus making it nearly impossible, if not illegal, for people to observe Communion in their homes. Churches were built, and the focus shifted from the people who gather to the place where they gather. Creeds were developed in an effort to expel heresy, but there was also a clear political motive: unify the empire. It is notable that Constantine is always in the center of fourth-century artwork depicting the Council of Nicaea.

During this time many Christians moved to the margins of the empire, into the desert, because they did not believe in a so-called Christian nation. Some of these desert fathers and mothers lived alone as hermits (eremitic), but many created communities (cenobitic). The first reference in Roman law to the desert monastics is in regard to them as tax resisters. Many were also considered war resisters or bandits, and some of the women had been notorious prostitutes before joining these desert communities. These desert fathers and mothers insisted on the primacy of love over knowledge, asceticism, prayer, or any other spiritual discipline. This was not a sentimental love but spiritual identification with one's brother and sister, taking one's neighbor as one's self. Vonetta and I were inspired by the practices of these early Christians and sought a return to these early practices.

In our pursuit and self-education of radical Christians and movements, we encountered Francis and Clare, Dorothy Day and the Catholic Worker Movement, Jean Vanier, Jesus People, and the most recent incarnation of Christian community in North America, New Monasticism. When Vonetta and I founded Radical Living, we had never heard of New Monasticism, but many people wanted to join us because they had read Shane Claiborne's *Irresistible Revolution* or had been learning about this movement in other ways. Though in some ways we still remain outside of and occasionally critical of movements like New Monasticism (or the emerging church), we clearly sensed that people were awakening, much as we had, to a new movement of the Spirit. It was a blessing to discover that others in the twenty-first century also felt this call to Christian community. We were glad to meet New Monastics such as Mark Van Steenwyk, Eliacin Rosario-Cruz, Karen Sloan, Shane Claiborne, and Jonathan Wilson-Hartgrove. We continue to steep ourselves in the words of our spiritual forebears to allow their rhythms to resonate into our lives. We understand that Christian community is not something new, that we have much to learn from others, yet we also understand that we are called to be faithful in our contribution to building communities.

Christian intentional communities need to be redemptive communities where all, regardless of ethnicity, national identity, or economic status, are invited to participate in the communal rhythm of Christian living. The current generation of progressive Christians has done amazing work in broadening the social agenda among evangelicals, Catholic, Anabaptist, and mainline Christians, but now it is time that we trust what our hearts and minds believe and actively pursue the reconciliation we talk about. The next step, rather than being a voice for the "voiceless," is to hand the microphone over to indigenous community leaders and ask them to facilitate the conversation so that we might grow and deepen in relationship with one another and with God.

Every one of us in this movement needs to plead with God to make us ministers of reconciliation. We must pray for eyes to see the structural racism perpetuated by unjust policies and a shared history of colonialism and slavery. Some of us will need to repent of inaction and empty rhetoric. Others simply need to heed what the Lord is already speaking to us. All of us will need to advocate affirmative action in our communal houses and actively pursue reconciliation.

We are hopeful that the Christian intentional community movement will be a diverse, Christ-centered, Spirit-led movement. And if all of us in this conversation will extend transparency, grace, and love to one another, we will surely disable the structural racism that has infected the church for far too long. And then we will be able to truly proclaim Jubilee!

Chapter 4

Bible as Radical Text

Indeed, the word of God is living and active, sharper than any two-edged sword, piercing until it divides soul from spirit, joints from marrow; it is able to judge the thoughts and intentions of the heart.

—Hebrews 4:12

I have always carried "bibles" of some sort with me during my travels. At seventeen, as I wandered the American West, my holy scrolls consisted of Walt Whitman's *Leaves of Grass* and T. S. Eliot's *The Wasteland*. A few years later, in Europe, India, and South America, my scrolls were the *Bhagavad Gita* and the Holy Bible. In Morocco, I read the Koran, but the text holy to me was the Bible, and the eighteenth century Samurai text *The Hagakure* was a close second.

I first read the Bible in its entirety as a nineteen-year-old backpacker in India. Although I was living with my Christian missionary aunt and uncle, I was still an idolater, in the most literal sense, and followed gods that reflected my desires rather than the holy will of the Most High. Just as I had read the Bhagavad Gita, Chaitanya Charitamrita, Srimad Bhagavatam, and other sacred texts while I was with the Hare Krishna, I now began to read the Bible while I was with Christian missionaries. I asked my uncle for a Bible, which he gladly gave me, suggesting that I begin in the New Testament, advice I now give to others beginning their first journey through the Scriptures. I immersed myself in the holy text, initially looking to scrutinize the book and find holes.

Each time I found something in a passage that troubled me (or that I thought could be used to subvert my missionary family's fundamentalist faith), I took it to my uncle. "Uncle Bruce," I said, "wasn't John the Baptist the *reincarnation* of Elijah the prophet? The Scriptures clearly say that John came in the 'power and spirit of Elijah'?" As soon as he responded, always with grace, wisdom, and warmth, I was on to the next text. "Uncle Bruce, didn't Paul write that women shouldn't speak in church? If they have questions, they should ask their husbands when they get home? I know that I saw Aunt Ruth Ann and Cousin Becky talking in church on Sunday morning." Question after question I asked, and always he took the time to explain each passage.

Eventually I softened; rather than scrutinizing the text for what it might be lacking, I began to seek the Scriptures for what they might offer. I read the Gospel with eyes toward Jesus, his ministerial vision and life. Removed from the dominant culture in which I was raised, my mind began to open to the beauty, mystery, and truth of Jesus' life. His humble birth and humiliating death awoke me to God's tenderness, and his compassion coupled with holy boldness gave me insight into God's character.

At Christmastime that year my mother sent me a gift of $100, and so I decided to take the nearly two-thousand–mile trip from the Nilgiri Mountains in Tamil Nadu to Himachal Pradesh in the Himalayas. The journey required several days in various buses and rickshaws, a three-day train ride, and another bus. I chose Manali as my destination because the *Lonely Planet* travel guide to India wrote about this mountain village: "Warning! Connoisseurs of marijuana frequent this region." This seemed to me to be more of an invitation than a warning.

On the final bus ride, I met a man named Johnny who managed a hotel in Manali. He said I should stay at his hotel and that my limited funds would not be an issue. When we arrived at his hotel, which was not luxury by any standards but did have a large bed, amazing view, and a small TV, I told him how much I could afford. "Impossible," he said, but hesitantly agreed to let me stay for one month for $30. I then pressed that I would also need meals. It appeared that he took me on almost as a charity case; or, more optimistically, he was an extender of hospitality to a teenager abroad. For the first week, I attempted to order chicken biryani and other meat dishes; each night I received a plate of naan (flatbread) and dahl (lentils) and a cup of tea. After that, Johnny did invite me to join his wife and newborn child once a week for a meat dinner.

I often ventured to other neighboring villages, such as Old Manali and Dharamsala, which is the capital of the Tibetan government-in-exile and the base of operations for the Dalai Lama, and even crossed into the politically divisive state of Jammu and Kashmir. I met sadhus, lamas, rinpoches, yogis, and ascetics, and became accustomed to joining a group of Shivaites who gathered in a circle to smoke charas (also called Manali hash). They sang *Alakh Bom*, and others responded *Bom Bom Shivaya*. A young Shivaite, not much older than I was, with matted hair coiled atop his head, three red stripes across his forehead, and ash covering much of his exposed body, befriended me and showed me to Arjuna's cave. He explained that this is the place where the hero of the Bhagavad Gita practiced *tapasya* (various ascetic and penitential exercises) to gain mystical powers.

I was smoking charas, but I also read the Bible. When I began the creation story in Genesis, either high from charas or enraptured by my encounter with the Word, I no longer felt as if I was reading the story but that the story seemed to unfold before me. It was as if light came into the darkness, order came from chaos, the heavens and the earth formed, gardens grew, and creatures were born.

My faith at the time was syncretic. I was a born-again singer of Hindu chants. I was encountering God through the Christian Scriptures, yet I was still immersed in Hindu pursuits of knowing the *Other*. From that point as I read the Bible, naïve yet sincere, I incorporated practices into my reading that I had learned from my time with Hare Krishna. I would allow myself to lose myself in the Scripture. At times I would stop reading, and prostrate myself on the floor in complete surrender to the One I was seeking. I would plead to God to speak to me, and perhaps through me. Although I thought these devotional practices were unique to the Bhakti expression of Hinduism, I later realized that these practices are actually quite Christian. It was during that first devotional reading of the Bible that I encountered God speaking to me. I encountered mystical revelation and union with God.

Lens of Perspective

It was through my lens of experience that I understood Scripture, and it was encouraging to see that God and the biblical authors were genuinely concerned for socially marginalized people. For example, the Bible often talks about exacting justice for the fatherless, which I interpreted as doing right by the single-mother households. The Gospels also spoke very clearly to my heart. When Jesus said that he came to bring good news to the poor, I interpreted this to mean that he did not just come to offer charity but to bring radical social change. *The last shall be first. The poor shall inherit the earth.* I grew up poor, as did my mother (and her mother), and through Jesus I was now heir to a Kingdom. Through Christ I gained an innate dignity on which the world could not place a value.

Each of us reads the Holy Scriptures through our unique perspective; and we carry our life experiences with us as we read, study, interpret, and attempt to apply their wisdom, teachings, and transformative power. The Word of God is alive. It is filled with mystery, beauty, and truth, and as we read the Word we should keep ourselves open to mystical possibility and holy expectation. The beauty of the Word gradually unfolds into our lives as we seek a glimpse of the face of God. When we approach the Holy Scriptures, we enter into conversation with the Author, yet we should remain conscious that there were also many authors and social-historical-political contexts in which the Scriptures were written.

In my pursuit of God I am continually reminded that my reading and understanding of the Scriptures is filtered through my lens of perspective, which in turn is shaped by relationships and life experiences. We focus on certain verses and passages and ignore other parts of the Bible. (Jesus did this, too.) The Word calls to be heard and hopes for its hearers to respond. By allowing my personal experiences and perspective to enter into conversation with the Scriptures and the Holy Spirit, my relationship with Jesus deepened. Much of the myths and cultural interpretations of Christ that I accepted as a young person fell away as I drew closer to the Lord, and yet even now, I need to continue to be on guard that I do not put myself before the God-self when reading Scriptures and seeking Jesus.

Jesus and the Bible

Jesus knew the Bible. He quoted Scriptures to those he taught as well as to Satan and the religious leaders of his day. He read the Bible in the synagogue, and his commentary on the Isaiah scroll enraged the congregation to attempt to kill him. Perhaps they became enraged because he strongly implied that the Gospel was *also* for those outside the covenant, such as Naaman the Syrian and the widow from Sidon, yet the fact that he consciously left out one part of a verse in his reading (a verse dealing with God's vengeance) may have initiated the congregation-turned-mob's desire to throw him from the brow of the cliff at the town's edge.

People want the Bible to speak to their experience. They want to be justified in their beliefs. That is one reason why folks go to church where people look like them, talk like them, and share the same cultural experience.

At Radical Living, the members who choose to attend a Sunday morning worship service are encouraged to join or participate in the life of a local church in the neighborhood. In Brooklyn, as in many urban centers, there are a wide variety of denominations located in each neighborhood, yet the cultural context is distinct. For example, in our neighborhood in Bedford-Stuyvesant, which is primarily African American and West Indian, there are Episcopalian, Baptist, Catholic, and many other types of churches. Thus people do not need to take a train ride into Manhattan to find a church that represents their doctrinal convictions or denominational affiliation.

A person who roots herself in a local church will be stretched and strengthened. There is a blessing in worshipping with neighbors and participating in service projects that directly address the needs of the neighborhood in which one lives and worships. To put it bluntly, "destination churches" are often more self-serving and entertainment oriented than neighborhood churches who are seeking to impact their communities with the lived Gospel.

Yet local churches are not without their own shortcomings. As we see with Jesus' return to his local congregation in Nazareth, at times local churches can also become insular and self-serving. Jesus' message of radical inclusivity was not received by those in his hometown congregation. We must stay open to the movement of the Spirit through the Word. If we remain flexible and open to the Word, we will discover that when we are stretched we will ultimately be strengthened in our faith.

Jesus was incredibly imaginative and inventive in his appropriation of terms and titles from the dominant culture. Terms, such as "apostle," "Son of God," "Gospel," and "church," were not terms he mined from the Hebrew Scriptures, but terms borrowed (or rather co-opted and subverted) from the Roman and Greek cultures that had dominated the region. *Apostle* was used by the Roman Empire for its emissaries. An apostle was a person sent to outposts of the empire to represent the empire's interests. Thus an apostle of Christ is a representative of the coming Kingdom in this world. *Son of God* was a title employed for the emperor. *Gospel* was a message of good news, reporting things such as the end of a war and the birth of the emperor's son. And *church* (*ekklesia*) was a Greek term describing a group of people who make decisions together, basically the smallest form of government.

These terms have lost the social and political punch they had upon their initial hearers, and thus much of the sociopolitical implications too are lost. The radical sentiments are lost over the centuries and millennia, and it must be our work to reclaim those original meanings, while living in the tension to make relevant the message for our current social and political context. And we should not allow those who most loudly and aggressively share their opinions, often under the guise of *historical fact* or *orthodoxy* or *fundamentalism*, to shape the conversation regarding biblical truths.

Jesus was critical of the scribes and Pharisees. The scribes were a group of professionals whose vocation was to copy and interpret religious texts, and the Jewish historian Josephus considered the Pharisees to be the most expert interpreters of the Torah. These people knew the Bible, but over and over again Jesus asks them, "Have you not read?" That might be akin to asking Christians today who claim to be a "Bible Christian" or "KJV-only Christian" if they've ever read the Bible they hold so dear. People may be able to quote the Bible, but if they fail to understand the deeper, more nuanced meanings of the Scriptures, they may miss the message. The Bible is used by too many as a stone with which they attack people or defend their position, when it is meant to be *bread* that nourishes and sustains.

Fishers of People

Jesus quoted Scripture, but rather than giving attribution to the book, chapter, and verse (which were later innovations), he allowed the Scriptures to speak through him. He was immersed in the text, and its language was his language. Some of the meanings of Jesus' language have changed, and our traditional interpretations of certain verses have even taken precedence over the original meaning of the passage.

Most children who spend any time in Sunday school will eventually draw a picture of a fish (perhaps placed in a frying pan or on a hook) with somewhere on the art project the verse "Follow me, and I will make you fish for people." The popular interpretation of this verse is used to support the important work of evangelism. And while I value genuine evangelism, I find that this passage is not calling people to be evangelists but to be prophets.

The context of this passage shows that John the Baptizer had recently been arrested, which caused Jesus to withdraw to Galilee. A grave injustice had just occurred. The prophet John was imprisoned, soon to be executed, at the whim of a ruler whom John accused of perversion and wickedness. Rather than admit his sin, he sought to suppress the voice of the one who cried in the wilderness, Repent! But that voice cannot be suppressed, because it is not John so much as it is God that spoke through John. It is at this time that Jesus called his first disciples, Peter and Andrew. He called them while preaching throughout the hill country: "Repent, for the kingdom of heaven has come near." We must ask, what happens to a fish when it is caught? The children's Sunday school lesson points us to the answer: the fish ends up on a hook and/or in a frying pan. Jesus' reference is to the prophets Jeremiah and Amos. Jeremiah prophesies: "I am now sending for many fishermen, says the Lord, and they shall catch them" (Jer. 16:16). And Amos prophesies even more directly,

> Hear this word, you cows of Bashan
>   who are on Mount Samaria,
> who oppress the poor, who crush the needy,
>   who say to their husbands, 'Bring something to drink!'
> The Lord God has sworn by his holiness:
>   The time is surely coming upon you,
> when they shall take you away with hooks,
>   even the last of you with fishhooks. (Amos 4:2)

A prophet points to injustice through words or actions, and then presents the new reality. A prophet understands the social history of his or her people, as well as the present cultural-political-spiritual context, and from that understanding is able to articulate a clear vision of the future. I believe that Jesus is calling prophets as much as evangelists, and the heart of the evangelistic message must be prophetic. I believe that Moses was sincere when he said he wished that all of the Lord's people were prophets (Num. 11:29). Those who claim to follow Christ must seek justice for the oppressed while proclaiming good news. The cry of the evangelist-prophet must be Jubilee!

Jubilee: The Heart of Jesus' Message

Jesus lays out his ministry platform in his hometown congregation in Nazareth by reading the first few verses of Isaiah 61. In this passage from Luke 4, Jesus reads a portion from Isaiah referencing the Holiness Codes (the "Jubilee passage") found in Leviticus. This is an incredibly deep text in that the Bible refers to itself three times (Luke 4; Isa. 61; Lev. 25). At the climax of the Lukan and Isaian passages, it reads that the freedom of prisoners, liberation of the oppressed, and healing of the brokenhearted is a result of the proclamation of "the year of the Lord's favor," which is also called Jubilee. Jesus is announcing that a new day is commencing.

Every seven years, the ancient Israelite community observed a Sabbath. During this time the earth was left to lie fallow and all agricultural activities ceased. The Bible and Israel have always had a deep connection to the land. The covenant between God and Israel is tied to the land, and thus much of their religious and cultural observances come from the people's relationship to the earth. The Jubilee occurred every seventh sabbatical year, but its implications far exceeded land regulations. During Jubilee, the land did lie fallow as in a regular Sabbath year, but there were also profound social implications. Family homes that were lost due to debt over the last fifty years were restored to the original families, debts were cancelled, and slaves were set free.

Today's market-based economy is a system that privileges those with the most capital to invest, often at the expense of those who have the least capital (and thus the least power in our capitalistic society). The Scriptures, including the Jubilee passage, are adamantly opposed to usury (the charging of interest on loans), specifically for the poor. In dozens of passages, the Bible rails against usury and exploitation of the poor, yet many Christians, and perhaps the American church as a whole, today fail to see this as a rallying cry to protect those on the bottom rungs of the economic ladder who are too often trampled by those who own the ladder. The American church is more prone to react than to act. Many argue that the government should stay out of economic matters, and allow the church to meet the needs of the poor. Sadly, while the church does do a great deal of work for the poor with food pantries and other services, she is not able to meet the needs of the growing underclass. Ironically, it is often those same people who argue that the government should stay out of economic matters who support ever-increasing military spending, tax cuts for the wealthy, and decreased services for the poor. It is also most often those same people who like to call America a "Christian nation" that also support cutting services for the poor.

With this understanding of Jubilee, we see that the spiritual and social are intertwined when Jesus proclaims, *The Spirit of the Lord is upon me. I have come to proclaim good news to the poor, set the captives free, restore sight to the blind, and liberate the oppressed.* For Christians today to proclaim Jubilee, we must create new systems and structures that benefit the poor and oppressed as well as confront the principalities and powers that exploit the poor and oppress those who dwell on the margins of society. We must stand with Jesus. When we stand with Jesus, we will see that we are standing with the poor, blind, criminal, and oppressed. It is they who will *hear* the good news when it is put into practice, when they experience Jubilee.

To follow Jesus means to value the Bible and to follow his way of interpreting Scripture. We are called to follow his teaching. Christians place great emphasis on doctrine, and many hold orthodoxy as the standard by which one's fidelity to Christ should be judged. Yet there are more than a few cases where some human doctrines (such as predestination versus freewill) have made their way into many churches while genuine biblical doctrines have been neglected (such as prohibitions on usury). Following Jesus means following his teachings, yet many Christians tend to spiritualize such teachings, particularly Jesus' Sermon on the Mount. If we were to accept these teachings as the right and true doctrine to the neglect of these extra teachings that do not directly impact the character of the Christian or one's relationship with others, we might find a deeper spirituality that has a fuller impact on society.

Who Wrote (and Interprets) the Bible?

Much of the Bible was written, edited, or redacted under the yoke of oppression. Many of the prophetic books were written under the threat of military aggression from a foreign power (such as Assyria and Babylon), and other texts were written during the periods of late exile or after exile, when the Jewish people were trying to reimagine their communal identity and how their God could exist apart from the temple. The exile (or captivity) was the practice of deportation of Jerusalem's elites by both the Assyrian and Babylonian Empires. The New Testament was written under Roman occupation and regularly employs the language of resistance and revolution, particularly in Jesus' announcement of the coming Kingdom and John's Revelation.

When we know whose side God is on, we know who the Bible is written for. The bulk of the Scriptures, Hebrew and Christian, were written by oppressed people for oppressed people. It was also written in, by, and for community. Understanding the contexts in which the Scriptures were written gives us insight into the character of God. It is in these creative tensions, in this liminality, that the nature of God is revealed. Jesus' choice to side with the poor, criminal, blind, and oppressed shows who it is that God chooses to speak to and through.

The sixty-six books of the Bible are divinely inspired—God-breathed. The Latin word *inspirare* contains the root of both the words inspire and respiration (that is, to breathe). The Bible is nothing but a lifeless letter unless the Spirit dwells in the person approaching the text. Karl Barth wrote that the Bible is not the Word of God but that it becomes the Word of God. Inconsistencies and contradictions open up to possibilities and promise. There are seeming contradictions in the Bible and an evolution in the understanding of God and God's relationship to creation and humanity.

Rather than seeing discrepancies between the synoptic Gospels (Matthew, Mark, and Luke), they are understood as three perspectives of humanity's encounter with the divine. To enter into conversation with the Scriptures we must strike a balance between reason and mystery.

Much of our understanding and interpretation of Scripture is informed by the (post) Enlightenment emphasis on reason and rationality, rather than embracing the mystery and beauty of God through the revelation of Scripture. While the European and American churches have been influenced by Enlightenment thinking, we in the West have much to learn from the Eastern (Byzantine, Coptic, Tawahedo, etc.) churches in regards to mystery. Awakening to how our cultural context shapes our worldview and interpretation of Scripture opens up new possibilities for understanding the Scriptures and thus enables us the opportunity for new encounters with God.

During the Reformation, Martin Luther espoused the doctrine of *sola scriptura* ("by Scripture alone"), the teaching that all that is needed for salvation is found in the Bible, and thus he was critical of church traditions. Nevertheless, much of Lutheran practice and liturgy remain rooted in these church traditions. Anabaptist radicals, such as Hutterites and Mennonites, were martyred in droves by Protestant (including Lutheran) and Catholic regimes during the sixteenth and seventeenth centuries, often because of their literal interpretation of Jesus' words. Tradition is essentially an established pattern of thought, action, or behavior. At times, Jesus opposed the traditionalists, but he also participated in tradition. Tradition has the possibility of strengthening or undermining the mission of the church.

The Anabaptists' interpretation of Jesus' teachings emphasizes absolute pacifism and nonviolence, which kept them from paying war taxes. Anabaptists were also opposed to taking oaths, since they attempted to follow Jesus' command to not make oaths, but to *let your yes be yes and no be no*. They were also noncreedal, which put them in opposition to the other church movements around them. Creeds were used by these other groups to expose heresy, but Anabaptists saw these creeds as unnecessary additions to Jesus' teachings. If ever Anabaptists had a creed, it might be argued that Jesus' Sermon on the Mount might serve that purpose. These biblical convictions resulted in arousing the suspicion of the local people and officials throughout the Western church, many of whom believed these Anabaptists were simply anarchists and, perhaps rightly so, counter to the dominant culture.

Rediscovering the Bible

The Bible's value for the cultures in which it has existed has often waxed and waned. An early example of this can be found during the reign of King Josiah (2 Kings 22) in Israel; carpenters, builders, and masons were hard at work restoring the temple when the Book of the Law, most likely the Torah, was discovered. The book was given to Hilkiah the High Priest who did not know what it was, even though he was the highest ranking religious professional. Hilkiah showed the book to Josiah who ripped his clothes as a sign of repentance and awe. Hilkiah then gathered other religious elites, who counseled that they should inquire of Huldah the prophetess, who also happened to be the keeper of the royal wardrobe.

Throughout the Bible, the people who rely on human wisdom, rituals, tradition, and mere religiosity are condemned, or at least closed to the presence of God, while those who depend on God and make themselves available to the Spirit are blessed by God's demonstration through them. In this case, the religious elites, all high-ranking men, had been confounded, but Huldah, a woman, understood the value of this sacred text. The Lord spoke through her to Josiah: "Because you have torn your clothes and wept before me, I also have heard you, says the Lord" (2 Kings 22:19b). Huldah was not in the inner circle of power, yet her prophetic gift was renowned; she was a woman in a world that often did not value women, yet God valued her immensely in that he spoke to her and through her. So too it is in our twenty-first century context. It is seldom the affluent and powerful who value or understand the Scriptures, but sometimes through those on the margins, all are given a glimpse of God's power. For example, it was largely through the witness of Martin Luther King Jr. that John F. Kennedy, and a nation, saw God's promise for an oppressed people break through. And yet it was an unsung twenty-two year old woman named Prathia Hall who wrote and first delivered the sermon "I Have a Dream." Just as Huldah is seldom known outside of Biblical studies circles, but may be credited for restoring the Scriptures to a place of prominence in the Jerusalem temple, so too Prathia Hall influenced a nation and generations of people through her prophetic message proclaimed by Dr. King on the steps of the Lincoln Memorial during the March on Washington in 1963.

Reading the Bible in Korea

Although I first read the Bible in India at the age of nineteen, I had moved far from my faith by the age of twenty-six. I was so far removed from attempting to live a life patterned after Christ that I found myself sitting in a Korean prison on drug charges. The only American in the prison, my cellmates—I was in a foreigners' cell—were Mongolian, Iranian, and ethnic Koreans from China. We became friends and played backgammon on a handmade backgammon board with pegs carved from soap. I petitioned the guards for a Bible, and after a couple of weeks they gave me a dual-language Korean-English Bible, which I read to pass the time. In my brokenness and desperation, my mind began to open, and my heart softened to the possibility that even in my captivity hope might return. It was in that mere *hope* that hope might return that my faith began to return. A few months later I was deported, and a year later in Brooklyn my faith returned in a way that has affected my life in significant ways, such as meeting the woman who would become my wife, forming an intentional community, and entering full-time ministry. Encountering the Bible with an open mind and soft heart opens up possibilities for a new life on an individual and collective level.

Critical and/or Devotional Reading of the Bible

The Bible must be read both critically and devotionally. The teachings of Jesus, as well as the stories of his life, death, and resurrection, are instrumental in walking with the Lord. It is important to read slowly and prayerfully, and study with others. There are many ways to read and understand the Scriptures. Understanding allegory and historical/

cultural criticism is helpful, especially when wrestling with questions such as the age of creation, or perhaps more practically how we should treat immigrants, or where to find hope in moments of suffering and brokenness.

The Scriptures contain historical narratives, poetry, and prophecy. Early Christians, particularly the writers of the New Testament, observed that all Scriptures point to Jesus. The transfiguration of Jesus points to the Christ as the fulfillment of the law and prophets. And while Jesus valued the Scriptures, he did not hold to an exclusively rigid interpretation of them; he was incredibly imaginative and insightful in how he revealed the heart of the message. So too should we approach the Scriptures with reverence and imagination.

It is important to approach the Word with reverence for God, trusting that those who wrote the Scriptures had encountered God and that the same Spirit that spoke to its writers may also speak to its readers. To enter into sacred time and space, we must pray before and after reading, and keep our mind open and heart tender to God. It is important to go regularly to the Word and carry the Word in our heart. We are not simply to read the Scriptures, but also meditate and pray through the Scriptures. We must read individually but also make time to wrestle with the Word communally. While studying the Scriptures, it is important to consider what passages of Scripture are essential to the faith community. Do any passages serve as obstacles or stumbling blocks; are some verses dangerous, ignored, or simply overlooked? We must approach the Bible with openness and an acceptance that we likely have more questions than answers and that God does still speak to and through those who call upon the name of the Holy One.

Chapter 5

Promise and Perils of Perpetual Revolution

O perpetual revolution of configured stars,
O perpetual recurrence of determined seasons,
O world of spring and autumn, birth and dying!
The endless cycle of idea and action,
Endless invention, endless experiment,
Brings knowledge of motion, but not of stillness;
Knowledge of speech, but not of silence;
Knowledge of words, and ignorance of the Word.
All our knowledge brings us nearer to our ignorance,
All our ignorance brings us nearer to death,
But nearness to death no nearer to God.
Where is the Life we have lost in living?
Where is the wisdom we have lost in knowledge?
Where is the knowledge we have lost in information?
The cycles of Heaven in twenty centuries
Bring us farther from God and nearer to the Dust.

—T. S. Eliot, *Choruses from the Rock*

We participate in rhythms that are sometimes sacred and other times profane, but mostly these rhythms—these seasons and cycles, revolutions, and recurrences—are mundane; they are the commonplace experiences of everyday existence. Too often we are merely passive participants in creation, moving with the ebb and flow of the circumstances in which we find ourselves. Yet in these rhythms of life we occasionally hope for a change to break up the humdrum and sometimes harmful patterns of life. We hope for a new rhythm to emerge—something that will allow deeper joy, peace, love, and satisfaction to enter into our lives.

Before this newness takes effect, there is often a stillness or silence—a time where we begin to awaken to the realization that we are in a cycle that leads to death and not life, despair and not hope, information and not knowledge, fear and not faith. The silence is not always our own. Sometimes it comes from outside of us. Yet, in the silence we wait; we yearn for the newness; we cry out in anticipation, joy, fear, anger. We realize that things do not have to remain the way they are. Another way is possible. A new idea or identity or path is about to be born. This silence is experienced individually but also collectively by communities, generations, and cultures.

This silence and yearning is evidenced in what is known as the intertestamental period. Between Malachi, the last book of the Hebrew Scriptures, and Matthew, the first book of the Christian Scriptures, there were four hundred years of silence without any prophetic voice. There had been religious teachers, such as the rabbis Hillel and Shammai, but like some of today's religious teachers, they debated the finer points of religion and too often followed their own social, religious, and political agendas rather than preach good news to the poor and share their lives with those on the margins. During the intertestamental period, there were also people of means, such as the Maccabees, who waged war against the Seleucids to restore Israel's independence as a nation. They waged war for an earthly kingdom that lasted less than one hundred years before the land and the people were again subjugated, first by the Greeks and then the Romans.

At the end of these four hundred years an elderly, barren woman named Elizabeth became pregnant with the one who would be called John the Baptizer. Elizabeth, unable to bear a child, was barren like Israel, who could not bear a prophet. Yet she birthed a prophet and the forerunner of the Messiah. The Scriptures mention John's birth but nothing of his childhood. And then suddenly they describe John the Baptizer, who came blazing across a sky filled with darkness. Jesus said that John was a "burning and shining lamp" and that "among those born of women no one has arisen greater than John the Baptist."

John the Baptizer lived in the wilderness eating locusts and wild honey and wearing a girdle of camel's hair. He had the favor of nobody. He had the Roman army and the Jewish aristocracy against him. He had the Pharisees and Sadducees against him. When the religious elites came to receive his baptism, he called them a brood of vipers. He had no possessions, and the Scriptures clearly say that John performed no miracles (John 10:41). He did not exorcise demons, restore sight to the blind, or heal the sick. Neither did he raise anyone from the dead. What he did do is proclaim the immanent arrival of the Messiah and the Kingdom of God.

In the wilderness, John had been seeking God, crying out to God and to others on God's behalf. He was immersed in the Holy Scriptures and knew that Isaiah had prophesied that one day a man should come in the wilderness crying, "Prepare the way of the Lord, make his paths straight." He knew that way would be called the way of holiness, and fools will not enter therein. John understood the importance of his message. He did not preach a self-centered message of self-help. He did not wax poetic or lose himself in philosophical musings. He preached a Christ-centered message of salvation. He proclaimed the coming Kingdom of peace and justice and righteousness. John counted the cost of fidelity to God and, in the end, paid the price with his life.

Repentance as Revolt

John was Jesus' cousin. They spent their entire lives under Roman occupation; they witnessed liberation movements, heard stories about those who made messianic claims as well as those who fought to remove the yoke of oppression placed upon them by Rome. They also saw those, such as tax collectors and tetrarchs, who benefited from cozying up to those in power. Jesus spent his formative years in Galilee, which was a hotbed of revolutionary activity.

There was Simon of Perea, who had been a slave of Herod the Great. Simon claimed to be messiah and king. He raised up many followers and, in revolutionary fervor, burned down the royal palace in Jericho. He met a quick demise when Herod's soldiers killed him and his followers in 4 BCE. A year later in 3 BCE, Athronges, an Israelite shepherd turned insurgent, was killed by the Romans for leading an uprising. Judas of Gamala, perhaps the most well-known insurgent, led a violent revolution against Rome in reaction to the heavy taxation placed upon the Galilean peasantry. Judas was killed in 6 CE. Jesus and John were surely familiar with these stories of first-century Jewish revolutionaries and purported messiahs. And although neither John nor Jesus advocated violent revolution, they were both murdered for their rhetoric, if not also their actions; Jesus executed under Roman law and John beheaded under Herod's regime. The violent revolutionaries are merely side notes in history, whereas John and Jesus, who never raised a sword or gave an order to kill, initiated a movement of peace and justice, hope and redemption, that is still alive today.

It was John who baptized Jesus in the Jordan River. And it was during Jesus' baptism that John receded and Jesus' ministry began. In the baptismal waters, the Spirit of God, in the form of a dove, descended upon Jesus. The Father tore open the heavens and said, "This is my Son, the Beloved, with whom I am well pleased." At that moment, in the baptismal waters, Jesus was commissioned by the Father and strengthened by the Spirit. It was that same Spirit that rested upon him as a dove that then drove him into the wilderness where he fasted and prayed, and was tempted but overcame. After he emerged from his wilderness experience, the Scriptures say he "began to preach and to say, 'Repent, for the kingdom of heaven is at hand.'" According to Matthew, these are the first words spoken by Jesus when he began his ministry, and on these first words hang the crux of his ministry.

The original Greek word for repentance is *metanoia*. It means a *change* or *overturning*. In the biblical context, repentance is twofold. It implies a turning from sin and turning toward God. It implies that we turn from our self-centered, sinful nature toward a Christ-centered, holy nature. The call to repent is the call to turn from our agendas, regardless of how altruistic they may be, toward God's plan for a new creation. On a personal level, it requires a change of attitude, but it also involves a shift in social practices. This is what John was talking about when he said to "bear fruit worthy of repentance." He was imagining new ways of using power and possessions.

Jesus, like John, preached the baptism of repentance for the remission of sins. He taught that repentance is more than merely apologizing. It is not just repenting for the sins you've done. It is repenting the motive that made you commit the sin. It is going past the fruit to the root, because if the root of corruption is there, the fruit that grows from it will be rotten. Repentance begins by renewing the inner person. As we have a change of heart and mind, our lifestyle corresponds to those changes. The revolution extends outward to redeem other circles in which we participate such as renewing and redeeming family relations, strengthening communities, neighborhoods, and the society in which we live, and, somehow, even redeeming the vast expanses of the cosmos—Paul wrote to the church in Corinth that all *creation groans for redemption.*

Preaching repentance and the coming Kingdom is political language. Repentance implies social change and the subversion of the dominant system. Christ was crucified explicitly for this subversive rhetoric. The Roman Empire crucified Christ, not because he was a miracle worker or turned over the tables in the temple, and not even because he counted himself equal with God (although this is the provocation that led the religious elites to seek Christ's death), but because he was considered a king in opposition to Caesar and talked about regime change. This is the charge that saw him crucified. This message of repentance and the coming Kingdom is an affront to the present world order. This language of change and overturning implies revolt. Revolt against the present order for a new Kingdom is on the horizon; revolt against the hopelessness and greed of the present system; revolt against selfishness, arrogance, and unforgiveness; revolt against measuring ourselves according to the standards of this world. In the Kingdom of God there is hope and justice and enough—enough food, enough resources, enough housing, enough love—for everyone.

When the devil took Jesus to a high mountain and tempted him with worldly political power, he was trying to co-opt Jesus' mission; he tried to give Jesus the corrupt worldly political system in an attempt to derail the Holy Kingdom, which ultimately requires every person, tribe, and nation to submit to its way of peace and justice and holiness. The Kingdom of God is different from all the present kingdoms, nations, and political and spiritual realities of today because, as the Word says, "the greatest among you must become like the youngest, and the leader like the one who serves" (Luke 22:26). It is a kingdom in which the poor, the hungry, those who mourn, and those who are hated are considered blessed; whereas the opposite is the case for the wealthy and content.

The Kingdom of God is breaking into this world, but the events of the old order continue to operate. Still the rich enjoy their wealth; still those who eat more than is necessary rejoice in their feasting; still news media is more interested in the powerful than in the weak. While many unwittingly live on earth as it is in hell, those who have heard the good news and respond to its call of discipleship and life transformation strive to live on earth as it is in heaven, and in turn share that good news, in word and action, with all who might hear.

In our current day, the coming Kingdom may not appear to pose much of a threat to the powers that be. The church has largely been co-opted by the American Dream, left and right politics, individualism, and exaltation of the self. Unfortunately, many American Christians look forward to heaven in the sky rather than seeking to build heaven on earth. There are very real powers and principalities that oppose God's Kingdom. It is not simply an ideological war.

There are very real battles occurring between angelic hosts and demonic forces. Before moving to New York, and before I was attempting to live a life faithful to Jesus' teachings, I was skeptical of claims of demonic possession. I have come to understand that there is a spectrum of perspectives on demons; some believe demons exist as evil spirits, mental disorders and addictions, or systems and structures. I have come to accept that demons exist in all these various forms. Demons rage in nations not with tails and pitchforks, but in manifestations that oppose the Kingdom. They represent an oppressive and destructive spirit in individuals, in society, and in the world. They war against the Kingdom of God, against God's beauty, truth, and mystery.

Jesus brought hope and healing to individuals, but he also came to overturn corrupt systems, to defeat the powers and principalities of this world, and to break down the gates of hell. In an act that might be perceived by some today as "Guerilla Theater," Jesus went into the temple and overturned the moneychangers' tables, accusing them of turning his Father's house into a den of thieves. By this act, he was also overturning a corrupt economic system that was bent on exploiting the poor, particularly in that the temple was unfairly giving bad exchange rates on the conversion from Roman coins to Jewish ones.

When Jesus arrived in the land of the Gadarenes, he met a demon-possessed man in the tombs. Jesus asked, "*What is your name?*" The man with broken chains on his wrists and ankles replied, *Legion. For we are many.* Legion is a Roman military term describing a unit of several thousand soldiers. Some theologians and scholars consider this story of Jesus exorcising demons from the man in the tombs as a metaphor that Christ and his Kingdom will exorcise the Romans, the foreign powers, from occupying the land and the people of Israel—just as people are oppressed by demons, so are lands occupied by oppressors. As we repent of personal sin, so too we must lament over the sins of the world, and we must participate in social repentance, lest we become compliant.

The Kingdom's Nearness

John the Baptizer and Jesus both preached, "Repent, for the Kingdom of God is *at hand*!" They both stressed the nearness of God and the coming Kingdom. Describing the Kingdom's geographic and spiritual proximity to us, Jesus said it is *near*, it is *at hand*, and it is *within you*. The Kingdom of God is both present, and it is breaking into this world. Because this world is upside down and hostile to God, it requires an overturning; it requires personal, social, and cosmic revolution. When a Kingdom (or government) claims sovereignty over other nations, those threatened nations will either rise up and prepare for war or surrender to the authority of the coming Kingdom. There is a very real difference between worldly empires and God's Kingdom. God's revolution is nonviolent and wins battles with imagination rather than military might. It requires beating swords into ploughshares; it requires turning weapons of war into garden tools; it requires turning that which was meant for destruction into that which is creative and life-giving.

There is not a single just government on this planet, yet in every nation on every continent there are people pledging allegiances to flags, governments, and political parties when they should be submitting to the sovereign God who reigns over all creation. Individuals, cities, and nations are all called to repentance, to turn toward God! The citizens of Nineveh repented upon hearing Jonah's prophecy and were saved. Martin Luther King Jr. prophetically preached that this nation must repent of its racism, segregation, and Jim Crow laws; and when the 1964 Civil Rights Act passed, this nation experienced a salvific moment. Although the Kingdom of God has not yet fully broken into this world, the dream of the prophet began to manifest, and we got a glimpse of the coming Kingdom.

John Howard Yoder, in *The Original Revolution*, wrote that "The promised coming change involves social and personal dimensions inseparably. This was John's and Jesus' agenda, but it is also ours. In Jesus' time as in ours the question of revolution, the judgment of God upon the present order and the imminent promise of another one, is the language in which the gospel must speak."

Jesus often spoke of newness—new heaven and earth, new creations. We are called to participate in this newness. To start, God promises to make us new creations and give us a new heart and new mind. And because we struggle, we must take on this spirit of repentance. It is not a false spirit in which we chastise and browbeat ourselves and others, but a right spirit in which we acknowledge that, at times, we do fall short and that God's grace is sufficient. Turning from sin and setting one's heart on the Lord is like turning the hands of a clock to the correct time. Unfortunately, most of our clocks do not keep time well, so we must continue to reset the clock. We must continue to turn to the Lord to redeem every area of our lives that we may become ministers of reconciliation, bringing hope, love, and redemption into the broken parts of our world. When Jesus sent his disciples into the world, he began a perpetual revolution that will not end until it is "on earth as it is in heaven." He has chosen to do this overturning and re-creating in partnership with his disciples.

Revolutionary Identities and Womanist Strategies

In the context of the United States, where state-sponsored racial terrorism continues, particularly in the appearance of the "New Jim Crow" and the school-to-prison pipeline, where gender inequity in the workplace pervades, where sexual minorities are still treated as second-class citizens, it is my conviction that a new wave of liberationists must arise to set right society's many wrongs. It is important that these liberationists come from the people experiencing the oppression, yet it seems to me that it is also vitally important that those who look like the oppressor and speak the language of the oppressor but have repented of their complicity with that destructive system join in the struggle for liberation.

Thus, my question as a straight white man in a country that privileges straight white men is this: how do those who benefit from unearned privileges effectively participate in this liberation movement? Is it possible or even appropriate for straight white men to employ womanist, mujerista, or other similar theologies, tools, ideas, and language to subvert dominant social constructs? What are the initial steps and/or practical applications for a person with so much privilege to work toward liberation? Rather than being a voice for the voiceless, how do I help to amplify the silenced and censored voices that seek to be heard—and not necessarily speak on behalf of others? How might straight white men identify with those on the margins and participate in the struggle for liberation and justice, healing and hope, without co-opting the movement and further subjugating those with whom they are attempting to work alongside? I am invested in the work of liberation, and feel drawn toward womanism in particular, for two very personal reasons.

First, I was born to an unwed teenage mother and spent my childhood moving from place to place, occasionally homeless, and as a witness to domestic violence. I experienced what James Cone, father of Black Liberation Theology, calls "ontological blackness." Although unable to articulate my situation, I felt oppression within the very core of my being.

My mom and I had been homeless during some of my middle school years. She had had a string of boyfriends who lacked character or integrity, but for a time she dated an

African American named Victor who was an artist. He was cool and kind and responsible, unlike the other men she dated. It was during that time that I started to learn about Martin Luther King Jr. I asked my grandparents what they thought of him since Dr. King was a Baptist like them. They did not like King and said that he was a whole other kind of Baptist. I was frustrated with their response and, sulking, thought that I would rather be King's kind of Baptist than their kind. He was prophetic and talked about dreams and visions and offered hope to the poor and marginalized. It was then, in the midst of my teen angst, that I rejected the Christian faith that was handed to me and still my soul longed for wholeness. I repented of Christianity, as I knew it, and began my journey.

Today, I find that revolutionary and subversive theologies speak more clearly to the Gospel message that I believe in. For example, I am drawn toward womanism, although I am a white male. Womanism is a theology whose most notable theologian may be Delores Williams. It is a theology that emerges from the black woman's experience and is in many ways a response to and critique of liberation theology. Womanism resonates more deeply with me than does feminism, as feminism emerged from the middle class, and only in the last few years have I entered into what is considered the middle class. For much of my early life I was surrounded by the poor, white women who live in trailer homes and subsidized apartments, and I have often lived in communities that are multicultural, not out of altruism, but out of economic necessity. Liberationist and womanist theologians have helped me to understand my own oppression, and have pushed me to search for the ways that I am complicit in the systemic oppression that seeks to disempower and destroy whole segments of society.

A second reason that I am invested in the work of liberation and feel drawn toward womanism is that my wife is Afro-Guyanese, and our children are entering into a world still fraught with rampant racism. Although my family does not suffer economic hardship, we live in a country in which the dominant culture continues to devalue people based on their ethnicity and ancestry, gender, economic status, and other identity markers. As a husband and father, how do I counter the dominant culture's narrative, how do I comfort and support, strengthen and undergird my wife when society seems to undermine the value of all who are not of European descent, and how do my wife and I raise our children's consciousness to develop a race and class analysis while equipping them with the skills and emotional intelligence to thrive in this oppressive society?

Although I was raised in poverty, I had the privilege of my whiteness and male gender. And while I did experience oppression due to my economic status, I still had a privileged position as a white American boy who would grow to be a white American man. As a child, I watched sitcoms whose idealized American family resembled me (well, at least my skin color). Almost all Hollywood blockbusters star a white male; and all superheroes are white men. I internalized all of this to feel somehow superior. I did not consider how young black or immigrant children or females felt watching these shows, or what effect it may have had on them. But now I am able to see through my children's eyes.

Recently, my five-year-old daughter asked me to read a book about the Holy Family that she got from the library.

She asked why they all look "peach-skinned." I responded by asking her why she thought they were peach-skinned. She replied that the artist was probably peach-skinned. I asked her what she thought of the artist making Jesus his own skin color. She replied that it was unfair. Despite my daughter's young age, she sensed the injustice of portraying the Holy Family after one's self, particularly as a homogenous white family that represents the dominant culture. My daughter was not able to see herself in the Holy Family, and this troubled her. So too should we be troubled when we do not see ourselves in images of the divine, especially when such images clearly have an agenda to elevate one people group and thus subjugate another.

We must address power structures through countermemory and imagination in order to subvert the dominant culture's imposed meanings of these figures that perpetuate racist notions. We must challenge the status quo's preconceived notions and biases, and present another perspective that uplifts those who have been kept down and include those who have been left out.

The works of black, Asian, Latin American, LGBTQ, and womanist liberationists have helped me to realize the coded world in which we live. When we hear terms like "white male" we do not think much, but when we hear "black male," we often think of crime and threats to extort money. When our eyes are open to the dominant culture's agenda, we can begin to see that our society values certain people and devalues others. We see that state-sponsored racial terrorism continues in our country. The "War on Drugs" is code for the war on black men. This is not to justify drug use or criminality but to show the gross injustice and disparity in the ways that laws target certain members of our society. For example, a white man who works on Wall Street whose illegal activities serve to increase his capital at the expense of destroying the economy will usually end up serving little or no jail time, while a black man caught with a small amount of drugs will likely serve serious time, earn a felony, and thus be barred from certain benefits in society (voting, access to public housing, employment opportunities).

Oppression is not related exclusively to race or ethnicity or sexual orientation, and while race and class, and to a lesser extent sexual orientation, are intrinsically related, it is the poor (those on the bottom rungs of the economic ladder) who are often systematically pushed to the margins of society simply for their lack of wealth as well as their limited access to resources and educational and vocational opportunities. The media and political pundits use terms like "middle-class values," implying that the lower classes and poor have an inferior value system and are inherently less moral than their middle-class counterparts. It is a fallacy and an outright lie to equate an economic system with a moral system. If it were true, then the wealthiest in society would be the most righteous and moral people on earth. And yet a recent study[1] at UC Berkeley shows that rich people are more likely to lie, cheat, and steal, and that privilege actually promotes dishonesty.

As a white man with citizenship in the United States, one of my main challenges as a follower of Jesus is to find ways to identify and surrender the power and unearned privileges I have gained through my race, gender, sexual

[1] http://greatergood.berkeley.edu/article/item/affluent_people_more_likely_to_be_scofflaws.

orientation, and citizenship, particularly those privileges that were gained at the expense of other people groups. If a straight white Christian man does not actively seek to identify with the marginalized and oppressed, he will easily find himself identified with the oppressor. Thus, to deepen in commitment to the way of Christ, straight white men must take a posture of continual repentance, in particular repenting of their complicity with white male supremacist society.

For those who identify with the dominant culture, and/or who benefit from privileges gained at the expense of other people groups, we must choose whether or not to side with Jesus and thus stand in solidarity with the poor and oppressed, documented and undocumented immigrants, sexual minorities and other marginalized groups, or stand with the oppressor—capitalistic systems that establish the personhood of corporations while dehumanizing the poor. We must decide whether we will give preference to the poor and oppressed, and thus share our skills, resources, life experience, homes, finances, and more to advance "the good news to the poor."

Choosing Identities

For Halloween 2013, Vonetta and I allowed our children, Chloe (age five) and Elgin (almost four), to choose their costumes. We gave them each five choices from a list. Chloe was almost Coco Chanel, but opted for the more vibrant Frida Kahlo (she looked stunning in red dress, turquoise jewelry, and unibrow). Elgin ultimately chose Che Guevara, which raised all sorts of ethical questions, particularly due to our family's Mennonite identity and commitment to peace and nonviolence. I had to ask myself, regardless of how high minded he claimed to be, why I included Che on the list? And why did Elgin, who is not even allowed to use water guns, choose a violent revolutionary? Well, we gave Elgin agency, and so we consented to him being Che, the Argentine doctor-turned-revolutionary. One of the persons on the list that Elgin did not choose was Cornel West. I imagined my son dressed in a black-and-white three-piece suit with a small silk scarf around his neck, and perhaps some makeup to make it look like he had a gap between his front teeth to enact that inimitable Cornel West smile. And while my daughter, whimsical and wise for five, has the Westian flair and outrageous extroversion more than my son, it is my son who exudes West's cool dignity.

And while West has influenced me even to the point that I considered dressing my son like him for Halloween, so too Delores Williams, bell hooks (who is not a womanist, but a black feminist), and others provide the possibility that my daughter may choose to imagine and reimagine her social location throughout her life. My wife is Afro-Guyanese, yet she also has Chinese-Indonesian and Amerindian in her DNA. My ancestors were Norwegian and Hutterite, which is a religio-ethnic group unto itself. My wife is from the South American continent, and I am from the North American continent. And our children were born in New York City. Our children are, in most senses of the word, postmodern. As they mature, they will have many identities that they may choose from. It is my wife and my hope that their main identity will be in Christ.

When I had children, I discovered that I had become more radical and more committed to causes that affected my family, yet I was also more cautious. I stood less often in protest lines outside of the Immigration and Customs Enforcement detention center, and more often explored ways to participate in movements, often as a board member of an organization or by hosting planning meetings, that proved strategic and hopefully more prone to effect deep change. Children have a way of radicalizing parents (and the reverse is surely just as true).

And so, as a father, I asked myself, how do my chosen identities affect my children's identity? For example, how much womanist God-talk should I employ for my son and daughter's sake? We do not have to choose between identities, but we can be whole persons in a fragmented society who speak from our experiences, histories, and self-identities. We choose who we are, and we choose from where we will speak.

I am thankful that there are voices like Cornel West, bell hooks, Delores Williams, and James Cone, as well as personalities like Frida Kahlo and Che Guevara, who found ways to express their art, their angst, their desire to overcome systems of domination and oppression through various means, including painting, scholarly endeavors, and, dare I say, even violent revolution. In our postmodern age, people do not tune in to the nine o'clock news on Channel 5 each evening. They gather news from various sources on the Internet and elsewhere. There is no one spiritual leader, such as Billy Graham, who speaks a message for all; rather we live in an increasingly pluralistic society with many voices and a variety of ways for those voices to be heard. And in our fragmented society, we must seek voices and other work to engage the dominant culture in an attempt to increase peace, justice, hope and liberation, and eventual reconciliation.

Chapter 6

Resisting Commodification, Assimilation, and Novelty

In your struggle against sin, you have not yet resisted to the point of shedding your blood.

—Hebrews 12:4

Power is a dynamic that affects both the earthly and heavenly realm. For the Christian, the perception of power (who has it, how it is obtained, how it is shared and abused) is based on many things, including one's life experiences, social status, and understanding of Jesus' teachings and example.

The refrain of the old Gospel song goes,
There is power, power, wonder-working power
In the blood of the Lamb;
There is power, power, wonder-working power
In the precious blood of the Lamb.

What does this power look like in practical terms? We know what the opposite of this "wonder-working power" looks like. The power of this world contradicts the power that Jesus spoke about; it contradicts the power of the cross and the blood that was shed on Calvary. Most people consider someone powerful if she or he has wealth or influence. Generals are considered powerful because they command armies. CEOs of multinational corporations are considered powerful because they influence economic trends. Everywhere we go we encounter modes of power; some power is healthy and uplifts people, whereas other types of power oppress and exploit people.

The Scriptures talk about the powers and principalities of this world. There are systems and structures that seek to dominate and marginalize whole groups. For example, in the United States, we see that men often, but not always, have more power than women; citizens have more power than immigrants, particularly those who are undocumented; those whose ancestors come from Europe often have more power than those whose ancestors come from Africa, Asia, or Latin America. All of us, if we consider for a moment, can recall a time when we felt powerful—perhaps when you got your first paycheck—and all of us can think of a time when we felt powerless—perhaps when someone has reminded you one too many times of personal failures.

Some people have done absolutely nothing to earn the power and privileges they have, particularly in regards to gender and ethnicity and even, albeit to a lesser extent, class status. What do we do with unearned power that has been gained at the expense of other people groups; what can we do with that power so that others will recognize that they are invited and included at God's table? It is important to start by laying at the foot of the cross the power that the world has given you through unjust means, allowing preconceived notions and judgments to pass away, so that a tender heart may pump new life into you, and letting old, oppressive ways die, so that a new life may emerge.

It is important to consider ways we use power on both individual and collective levels. Is our power aligned more with the way of the world or the Kingdom of God? Jesus teaches us how to exercise power. He said to his disciples, do not *lord your power over others*, instead "Whoever wishes to be great among you must be your servant, and whoever wishes to be first among you must be your slave" (Matt. 20:26–27).

We are to use our power to come under those who suffer and struggle and lift them up, as Jesus did for us. How does it look in real life? Some have taken in a foster child, or mentored a young person from a single-family home, or volunteered on a consistent basis at an immigration clinic or a rescue mission. Some begin by investing (financially, emotionally, personally) into a local project or community activity.

This is the church, the manifestation of Christ dwelling among and within us. We get so distracted sometimes that we forget what the church is and what it is not. Returning to the foundational understanding that the church is the living, breathing body of Christ, we remember that each of us are living stones. We are cut and shaped and fitted together to be held by some and to uphold others. This is the church that God wants to inhabit, a people sharing life together, being vulnerable, taking risks, and trusting one another for support. And it is in this community of faith, deeply rooted in Christ's teaching and example, where God dwells.

Recognizing True Power

Some of us, particularly those who have been devalued by society, no longer recognize the power that we have within us. Regardless of how powerless some of us may think we are, Jesus says that *The Kingdom of God is within you*. There's something bigger than each of us inside of us, and it is waiting to break forth, a Holy Kingdom, the promise of another way, hope, healing, peace, and justice.

The resurrection is about transcending the current order, overturning the ways of this world, and beginning again. Yet, sadly, there are often times when we deny Christ's resurrection. We deny the resurrection when we choose to participate in culture wars rather than the life of Christ; when we blame the poor and oppressed for their situation rather than look deeper for underlying causes; we reject the resurrection when we participate in social and economic systems that dominate whole segments of society.

The resurrection is spiritual, but it also has legs; it is real, tangible. You can see it in the lives of those who have been transformed by following Jesus to the cross and then to the tomb. As followers of Christ, we begin to recognize our true identity as children of God. The reality of who we are called to be gradually unfolds as we enter more fully into eternity. The lies that the world espouses—that you have to earn this much a year to be successful, or your value comes from your physical appearance, or any other such nonsense—are seen for what they are: lies.

The lies and hypocrisy of the world are broken by the power of the resurrection. We realize that even if we did not have a good childhood, even if we have had a rough life, or are considered a failure by some (or perhaps many), we are in good company. We are in the company of Jesus, who also did not have it so easy, who chose to condescend to our brokenness and poverty so that we could relate to our Holy Father. Jesus, as the Second Person of the Holy Trinity, could have chosen to be born in the heights of power; instead he was born in a barn, he spent his first night sleeping in a trough, and he was raised in an occupied territory.

Jesus was persecuted by society and the upstanding religious types; they attacked him with stones; they questioned his legitimacy. And when they discovered this humble man of modest means had Godly strength and purpose, they sought to kill him. They stripped him naked, spit in his face, pulled the hair of his beard out by the handful, whipped him with a scourge, and counted him a curse. They turned him over to the authorities who in turn nailed him to a cross and executed him.

Christ could have called down angels to destroy the Romans, but as Peter wrote, "When [Jesus] was abused, he did not return abuse; when he suffered, he did not threaten; but he entrusted himself to the one who judges justly" (1 Pet. 2:23). Know this: It was not the Jewish aristocracy or the Roman powerbrokers who judged justly; it was God. The religious leaders may have sought his death, and the government may have sanctioned his execution, but the world does not have the last word. Christ was crucified, but on that third day, the tomb was found empty; this Jewish peasant was raised again, and the resurrection of a peasant means that empire will never have the last word.

Humility as Participation

Humility, which is the overturning of the world's concept of power, even extends to the heavenly realm. When John the Revelator ascended to heaven, there was a scroll that nobody was strong enough to open. And then a mighty angel proclaimed, "See, the Lion of the tribe of Judah, the Root of David, has conquered." But when John looked at the throne of God, rather than a mighty lion, he saw a slain and bloody lamb sitting on that holy throne. What may appear weak in this world reveals itself in heaven as Godly strength and holy purpose. What we may perceive as weak and powerless in this fleeting world has the potential to have mighty power in the eternal realm.

Humility is not a sign of weakness; it is a sign of Godly strength. Andrew Murray, the nineteenth-century South African minister, wrote that humility before others "will be the only sufficient proof that our humility before God is real . . . [The stresses of daily life] are the tests of eternity, because they prove what really is the spirit that possesses us."

Humility is our participation in the life of Jesus. As we know, not Jesus' birth and upbringing, not what the upstanding religious folks said about him, not even that deadly cross, had the last word. We know that on that third day, he rose again. The resurrection is the celebration of God's power over sin and death; it is resistance to the current order of domination and death; it is restoring power to its proper place; it is the celebration of the new life in Christ that each of us is invited to participate in. On that third day, God gave life where there once was death; he breathed when there was no breath left. And that resurrection power is still available to each of us today.

Empire, Exodus, Exile

Civilization's constructs of empire, exodus, and exile are evident throughout the Scriptures. The Bible was written almost exclusively by people suffering under the yoke of oppression. Many texts were written by people who were seeking a renewal of their communal identity after experiencing the trauma of exile; some texts were written in remembrance of how the Hebrew slaves were treated in Egypt and serve as a call to exercise hospitality to the immigrant. The writers of the Bible needed to know how to navigate under empire and understood the importance of seeking a way of exploring new identity in the midst of oppression. These stories have spoken powerfully to the experiences of people throughout history by providing comfort to those who suffer under a dominant culture, and providing a critique of the systems and powers that serve to dominate and oppress underrepresented groups. Unfortunately, today most Christians identify more with empire (rampant consumerism, militarism, and more) than with those who suffer from the consequences of empire.

Empire, exodus, and exile are interrelated in the Bible. The Hebrew slaves, after great struggle, chose the challenges and risks of exodus as opposed to the oppression of the Egyptian empire. The Israelites were forcibly removed from their homeland by the Babylonians and also by the Assyrians, who later allowed them to return to their homeland. Jesus and the first-century Jews also suffered under the Romans.

An empire is an extensive territory under single domination. It has military bases in regions in which it maintains vested interest, particularly in regard to resources it wants to control, governs by force, and promotes rhetoric of allegiance and nationalistic pride. Examples of empire in Scripture include Egypt, Babylon, and Rome; in modernity, examples include the United States, Great Britain, and to a larger extent economic regions and systems such as the Global North and capitalism.

An exodus is a mass departure that is fostered by an economic and political situation that forces a disenfranchised or enslaved people to move from one geographic location where they suffered to another, often unknown location. Examples of exodus include Israel, who wandered the Sinai Peninsula; the Tibetans who fled their homeland in the 1959 Chinese invasion; and the forced removal of the Cherokee, Creek, Seminole, Chickasaw, and Choctaw tribes in the United States, which resulted in the Trail of Tears.

An exile is a period of forced or voluntary absence from one's own home or country. Examples of exile include the Jews who were deported by the Babylonian king Nebuchadnezzar, the one million Cubans who have emigrated since the Cuban Revolution, and the Tibetan government-in-exile in Dharmsala, India.

The exodus story of the Hebrew people is perhaps one of the most well-known stories of a freedom movement in world history. The story begins with an enslaved Israelite community who "groaned under their slavery" and cried out to their God (Exod. 2:23–25). God heard their groaning and remembered his covenant with Abraham, Isaac, and Jacob. In the midst of the plagues, Israel disengaged from the empire and the false promises of Pharaoh. Israel petitioned Pharaoh no more and recognized that the empire would never liberate them. This total rejection of empire led to its dismantling. At the end of this narrative, Egypt released a death cry as a sign that the empire could not stand. "Pharaoh arose in the night, he and all his officials and all the Egyptians; and there was a loud cry in Egypt, for there was not a house without someone dead" (Exod. 12:30). Walter Brueggemann wrote in *Prophetic Imagination*, "The empire is left to grieve over its days of not caring and its gods of order, and its politics of injustice, which are all now ended."[1] Moses does not call the empire to repentance, he seeks to dismantle it entirely.

Brueggeman also notes Solomon's reign in Israel looked like other empires. "He had traded a vision of freedom for the reality of security . . . he had replaced covenanting with consuming. During Solomon's reign, tax districts displaced tribes (1 Kings 4:7–19) and a standing army was installed so that armaments no longer depended on public opinion and national interest (1 Kings 4:4; 9:22), not to mention the notion of the rush of God's Spirit."[2]

Empire is good at management but fails at compassion. Empire is good at regulating charities but unable to stand in solidarity with the poor and oppressed. Empires live by numbness. Empires, in their exercise of militarism, expect numbness about the human cost of war. Corporate economies expect blindness to the cost in terms of poverty and exploitation. We are all children of empire, committed to it in one way or another. So, how can we imagine a new reality?

First, we can explore ways in which our churches today challenge or might challenge us to critique the dominant

---

[1] Walter Brueggemann, *The Prophetic Imagination,* 2nd ed. (Minneapolis: Augsburg Fortress, 2001), 13–14.

[2] Ibid., 33.

ideology of our communities, cities, and nation. We can explore ways in which our churches are, or should be, living into the new reality of a more just, peaceful, and loving world. Do we perpetuate a politics of oppression in which the cries of the poor and disenfranchised are ignored or dismissed as the noises of outsiders? Can we explore ways in which our churches today enable or might enable the public processing of pain in the face of local, national, and global oppression, exploitation, and injustice?

Resisting the Empire

A group of people committed to overthrowing a foreign or occupying power may be referred to as a resistance. What power occupies or dominates our world? We must resist temptation—the temptation to acquire worldly power, to find security in possessions (which is a form of idolatry, and often leads us into debt); we must resist the temptation to seek social status, to participate in a system that exploits people.

When we look at the Scriptures we see many examples of resistance movements and movement leaders. For example, Moses, who was born in slavery but raised as royalty with great privileges and access to power, chose to identify with the Hebrew slaves rather than the royal Egyptian court. And we must consider who Jesus chose to identify with—the Roman Empire and the religious elite or the poor, sick, and socially marginalized—and why? Was Jesus concerned with managing the occupation or liberating the occupied?

Liberation theologians often employ the exodus narrative as the source story to empower disenfranchised groups. James Cone uses the story to empower African Americans to identify their oppressor and equip them to seek to separate from and overcome the dominant culture. Yet, Native American post-Christian theologian Robert Allen Warrior finds the exodus narrative to be an unacceptable model for liberation of indigenous peoples in this country. Warrior, an Osage from Oklahoma, argues that the traditional perspective of Yahweh as the deliverer of the Hebrew slaves becomes, for him as a Native American with "Canaanite eyes," the story of Yahweh the conqueror as the Hebrew people enter into the land of the Canaanite, Hittites, and Amorites, and believe that it is their land. Warrior and other Native American theologians, such as Vine Deloria, argue that this exegesis of the exodus narrative supports and helps to perpetuate Western notions such as manifest destiny. We must maintain a critical eye when interpreting and applying Scripture. When we participate in and learn from various resistance movements, we increase our sensitivity toward those who are affected by the struggle.

Boar Hunting with Berbers

Shortly after graduating from UW-Madison with a degree in international studies, I found myself in Morocco. I say that I *found* myself in Morocco because when I boarded that Boeing in Chicago headed toward Amsterdam, I never intended to go to Africa. As I mentioned earlier, my initial intent was to spend a few weeks in the Netherlands with Dutch friends and then venture to Eastern Europe with the hope of writing for an English-language, ex-pat newspaper such as the *Warsaw Voice* or the *Prague Post*. The stark realization of what it would be like to spend a winter in Eastern Europe convinced me to travel south, across the

Gibraltar Strait, to seek comfort in the warmer climes of North Africa. Thus I rode several days by bus and then took a short ferry ride to Morocco.

In Cascades d'Ouzoud (Waterfalls of the Olive Trees) in the Atlas Mountains of Morocco, I encountered an indigenous people resistant to empire. It was the season to gather olives to make oil, and people from distant villages had arrived to purchase the oil. Ouzoud had premium olive oil due to its high altitude and its proximity to an abundant water supply. The majesty of Ouzoud's waterfalls, the wildness of the Barbary apes clinging to the cliff face in early morn, and the evening revelries around a fire compelled me to stay longer than I had originally planned. I stayed in Ouzoud for more than a month and resided in a small room located halfway down the mountain and positioned twenty meters from the main fall. Every night the constant rumble eased me to sleep, and in the morning the rumble gradually turned into a roar until I was awake sipping mint tea and dipping flat bread into a small bowl of oil for breakfast. This was my rhythm.

One night as I sat in a small drum circle composed of European and Moroccan tourists, as well as many locals, Mahmoud, whose uncle owned the abode where I slept, as well as a nearby olive orchard, invited me to join him and a small band of his kin on a boar hunt. I asked, "Aren't you a Muslim?" When he said yes, I asked, "Then how do you plan to eat the boar?" "I was Berber before I was Muslim," he replied. And with that reasoning, off we went into the dark mountain forest. One man caught the trail of a boar and we chased it for nearly two hours until we were sweating and out of breath. "Not tonight," Mahmoud finally said.

We were far from Ouzoud, and so instead of turning back, we continued along the river until we came to a lone, isolated home with chickens and a ewe in the enclosed entrance. It was in the deep of night, and so I was surprised to see that his uncle's house was alive with activity. There was music within the house and many people who Mahmoud explained were his extended family. Old men and women were smoking kif, and children slept under blankets on kilim rugs. Mahmoud's uncle handed me a plastic bottle with suspect contents and said, "Berber whiskey." It was strong and immediately warmed my belly. He later explained it was fig schnapps he had made.

Surprised to see the uncle not only drinking alcohol but making his own schnapps, I asked him the same question I had asked his nephew earlier, "I thought you were Muslim." He responded, like his nephew, that they were Berber first. He explained that Berbers have been in North Africa for more than ten thousand years and that first it was the Arab colonizers and then the Europeans who attempted to uproot and destroy his culture through the propaganda of popular music and movies, which are even more devastating and subversive to culture than official government policy. He explained that Berbers are defiant. He said, "Arabic is my second language, French my third and English my fourth. Berber is my first language. It is the language in which I pray and thus it is my first identity." Mahmoud explained how Muslims had conquered the Maghreb, Northwest Africa, but that the Berbers revolted and even today maintain vestiges of cultural resistance and are thus able to maintain much of their indigenous identity. The parallels of Christian and Muslim colonization struck me, but the spirit of resistance moved me even deeper.

Commodification of "WWJD"

The Christian faith in the United States has become a product to be marketed. Senior pastors and church planters study church growth models and target certain segments of society in an attempt to attract them to their church. The terms "pastor" and "CEO" are sometimes used interchangeably. Conversations around budgets and capital development projects usurp deep prayer and communal devotions. The church is branded. This can be clearly seen with the commodification of the expression "WWJD" (What Would Jesus Do?). These four letters can be found on bracelets, bookmarks, bumper stickers, and T-shirts. The saying is taken from the alternate title of Charles Sheldon's book, *In His Steps*, written in 1897, which tells the story of a homeless, unemployed man who enters a church and charges that the congregants are apathetic toward the plight of the downtrodden. The man then suddenly and dramatically falls dead. Shaken by the event, the pastor of the church, at the following Sunday service, challenges his congregants to ask themselves before doing anything, "What would Jesus do?"[3]

This question was an authentic exploration into what it means to follow Jesus. Over time, this question was parodied, branded, and sold. Today there are few social implications for those who advertise WWJD, but the man who

[3] Charles M. Sheldon, *In His Steps* (New York: Sheldon Books, 2012), 9.

wrote the book, Charles Sheldon, was a leader in the Social Gospel Movement and was an advocate of Christian Socialism. Sheldon was not seeking to open a discussion on the topic of personal salvation with his question, he was challenging the response of Christians to poverty, unemployment, and to those who live on the margins of society.

The modern capital-driven branding and marketing of WWJD undermines the spirit of Sheldon's call to the church to serve, work in solidarity with, and advocate on behalf of the poor and oppressed. Christians are called to challenge the status quo, to question preconceived notions and biases regarding economic systems, and to explore authentic ways of bringing good news to the poor.

During my ordination process in the Mennonite Church, there came a point where I had to meet with the council of bishops (also called oversight ministers in my conference) to share with them my calling and respond to any questions they may have. I shared my vision of living in community, and how I believed that the institutional church in this country is changing, and that new models (some of which are actually ancient models) of church are emerging. My emphasis on communal identity in contrast to individualism struck a chord with some of them. One bishop asked me, not as an inquisition but merely as a means to identify my political position, "You sound like a Marxist. Are you a communist?" I replied that I do not consider myself a communist or a capitalist, and believe that through the power of Christ there is potential to redeem economic systems, although some systems that are too entrenched with exploitation must be discredited and completely dismantled. What is the goal of economic systems? Is it to create a system that benefits only a few, or is it to make a way in which the poor are not abandoned, but that their needs are met?

Disrupting Economies

To follow Jesus means that sometimes we must disrupt economies. For example, Jesus disrupted the local economy in his overturning of the moneychangers' tables in the temple, where he symbolically overturns a corrupt economic system that exploited the poor.

Another example is the story of Paul and the silversmiths in Ephesus. We read in Acts 19:23–27,

> About that time no little disturbance broke out concerning the Way. A man named Demetrius, a silversmith who made silver shrines of Artemis, brought no little business to the artisans. These he gathered together, with the workers of the same trade, and said, "Men, you know that we get our wealth from this business. You also see and hear that not only in Ephesus but in almost the whole of Asia this Paul has persuaded and drawn away a considerable number of people by saying that gods made with hands are not gods. And there is danger not only that this trade of ours may come into disrepute but also that the temple of the great goddess Artemis will be scorned, and she will be deprived of her majesty that brought all Asia and the world to worship her."

A riot ensued and, although Paul wanted to speak to the riotous crowd and make a defense of the faith, his friends encouraged him not to venture into the mob. Christians are called to take risks, to affect economies, and to create new ways to live life, share resources, and build one another up. In the midst of ushering in the Kingdom of God, we must maintain a resistance to the dominant culture. The church is to influence and participate in the culture, but not to be co-opted by it. For too long the church has struggled to wade into the deep waters of faith and has chosen to remain in the shallow end. We must recognize our shortcomings (aging youth ministers with soul patches, hipster preachers who focus on form more than substance, congregants who only see one another on Sunday morning), and explore new ways of deepening as a body (shifting the church culture from focus on the individual to focus on the collective, embracing interdependence). To resist the dominant culture, it is helpful to return to the original texts, the Scriptures, to learn how first-century Christians navigated empire, and to explore the stories they shared to shape their identity and to strengthen their resolve to resist the oppression placed upon them.

Models of Resistance

The first Christian communities were birthed in the backwaters of the Roman Empire. As the Christian movement spread to major urban centers in the Roman Empire, participants in this movement soon realized that to survive in the shadow of empire and resist the dominant culture, they needed to exercise a subversive imagination, a radical creativity that not only responded to the culture around them, but promoted new possibilities of hope for a people on the margins of society.

The first-century Jewish Christians were certainly a marginal people in the Roman Empire. Almost none were afforded citizenship, which would have provided them protection from sporadic yet widespread state-imposed terror. Like all other peasants and urban poor, they were subject to heavy taxation by the state and exploitation by government officials such as tax collectors. They suffered under crushing poverty. And apart from sporadic persecution and economic exploitation, participants in these new Christian communities also found themselves to be a concern for Rome, particularly in that they had deified a Roman political prisoner who was hanged on a Roman cross, a mode of execution reserved exclusively for insurrectionists. Their Savior was executed as a criminal, and thus those who modeled their lives on his teachings caused genuine concern among the authorities.

So, how did participants in this new movement negotiate their social location in the midst of empire? How did these radicals who were stripping away the pretenses of their tradition and worshiping a Revolutionary Savior operate in a world suspicious of their motives? We get glimpses to the ways these communities responded to empire and promoted new possibilities of hope throughout the Christian Scriptures, particularly in the epistles. The Christian Scriptures are unique among religious literature in that they consist mostly of letters addressed to new, and often struggling, Christian communities. These communities were far from a monolithic, homogenous people. These people represented a pluralistic movement consisting of people from a wide range of social, cultural, and economic locations. They were exceedingly diverse in their challenges, practices, and approach to the culture around them. These communities had little or no influence in the Roman Empire, and yet these groups of people who gathered in homes and public spaces to worship this Risen Christ were taking initial steps toward a revolutionary movement rooted in reimagining the social order.

It may be said that first-century believers, just as twenty-first century Christians today, discovered the challenge of leaving privilege. James, the brother of Jesus, wrote, "Listen, my beloved brothers and sisters. Has not God chosen the poor in the world to be rich in faith and to be heirs of the kingdom that he has promised to those who love him? But you have dishonored the poor. Is it not the rich who oppress you? Is it not they who drag you into court?" (James 2:5–6). There was a preferential option for the poor even in the first century. And it was in community and during these meals that early Christians experimented with a new social understanding of themselves. All were included, men and women, poor and rich, young and elderly, slave and slave-owner, and it was in this context that these communities experimented with utopian expressions of what they imagined what *on earth as it is in heaven* might actually look like in our world.

In times of oppression and persecution, suffering and poverty, people are forced to be creative in order simply to survive. The first Christians had to exercise their imaginations in order to negotiate their reality in the empire, not only to resist their oppression, but also to imagine other possibilities. Imagination was essential to participants in this movement, and the concept of *imagination* was rooted in their Holy Scriptures. The author of Genesis makes the bold claim that humankind is made in the *image* of God (Gen. 1:27). Thus we are made in the *imagination* of God. We derive from that creative, life-giving force. And from this imaginative, creative process we too are indwelled with great capacity to imagine and create new possibilities, hope in the midst of despair, and even life where there once was death. Because the poor and oppressed have limited resources they must make due with what is already part of their reality, such as language, relationships, and shared values.

Meals as Resistance

The meal was the common place for participants in this new movement to exercise new language (or reimagined language), shared values, and a reimagining of the social order. Meals were essential to Jesus' ministry as well as to the life of the early church as described in the New Testament. Jesus taught avidly at meals, and the teachings of first-century church leaders were almost always based around meals in community. The central activity of the church for the first few centuries was the shared meal (also called the Eucharist, Communion, or Agape Feast).

This meal was far different from the wafer cookie and thimble of grape juice that passes for the Eucharist in most traditions today. In the first few centuries it was a genuine meal, and participation was inclusive. Paul wrote to the church in Corinth: "When you come together, each one has a hymn, a lesson, a revelation, a tongue, or an interpretation. Let all things be done for building up" (1 Cor. 14:26). It was often during meals that the letters of the apostles were read, hymns were sung, and prophesies were proclaimed.

Yet early Christian meal forms were not formed in isolation. There were inevitable Hellenistic influences that shaped, at least in part, how these communities gathered (meal forms, models of decision making). Many of the associations, guilds, and religious congregations (such as those devoted to Demeter or Dionysus) of the Roman Empire were formed during the preceding Hellenistic Period, and it was during this time that the meal form began to flourish among the general populace. An early name for the church was taken from the Greek word for association: *ekklesia*. The central activity of many of these groups was the shared meal. These associations and guilds were formed around various identity markers, ranging from ethnicity and culture, economic status, religious orientation, profession, and others. At these Hellenistic meals women and slaves often served in leadership roles, thus experimenting with a changed social order focused on shared values.

Many of the patrons of the early church were women, and it was often in women's homes that the church gathered. All were included, and participation and leadership were not reserved exclusively for wealthy males. Yet we know that during these gatherings conflict did arise. Paul had to correct the church for getting drunk during this meal, and he also rebuked some for eating their fill while others went hungry. Paul writes, "When you come together, it is not really to eat the Lord's supper. For when the time comes to eat, each of you goes ahead with your own supper, and one goes hungry and another becomes drunk. What! Do you not have homes to eat and drink in? Or do you show contempt for the church of God and humiliate those who have nothing?" (1 Cor. 11:20–22a).

These meals were not the place to reinforce the biases and privileged positions already established in society. They were places to subvert dominant practices with new social values, to envision and practice the Kingdom of God *on earth as it is in heaven*, and to live as a model for what society might become.

Paul and Eutychus

There are many examples of Christian communities gathering for meals throughout the New Testament. One particular story that combines sharing a meal with spiritual teaching, a common motif in the Scriptures, is found in Acts 20. The passage states, "On the first day of the week, when we met to break bread, Paul was holding a discussion with them; since he intended to leave the next day, he continued speaking until midnight." Paul was in the midst of a missionary journey and had stopped in Troas, a region in what is today northwestern Turkey, to spend seven days encouraging the community there and regrouping with his fellow travelers with whom he was separated due to the riot he incited among the silversmiths in Ephesus.

This story begins on Paul's last day in Troas, and because he has such a desire to encourage them with the Gospel, he teaches late into the night. These gatherings had a semblance of structure, yet they were far removed from later liturgical developments. We see that throughout the New Testament the gathering often included singing, a shared meal, and a teaching, and at times prophecy, exhortation, and speaking in tongues. The people often gathered in a home that was large enough to accommodate a sizable group. The passage continues, "There were many lamps in the room upstairs where we were meeting." And later we learn that the house is three stories—a fairly large house for the first century.

It is around this time in the passage that we are introduced to a young man named Eutychus. Young Eutychus, likely a local from Troas inspired by the stories of Jesus that were circulating throughout the Mediterranean, was present to hear the words of the apostle Paul; yet as he perched in a window, he fell into a deep sleep. The Scriptures strongly imply that he was lulled into this deep sleep "as Paul talked on and on."

After Eutychus falls asleep, he falls three stories to the floor and dies. Paul then takes a break from preaching and goes to Eutychus and miraculously raises him from the dead. It is at this point that Paul went "upstairs again and broke bread and ate." And after the miracle and the breaking of bread, Paul "continued to converse with them until dawn." The Scriptures give us no hint what Paul was speaking about. Likely, he was providing this community with spiritual direction, sharing with them stories from his missionary adventures, and encouraging them with the Gospel. Yet all we learn after this whole ordeal is that the people "had taken the boy away alive and were not a little comforted." These people may have been as greatly relieved at Paul's departure as were the silversmiths in Ephesus.

Movie Night with Radical Living

Like the first-century church, the most common form of gathering at our Radical Living community is sharing a meal together. In our rhythm, we do have times for prayer and worship, the study of Scripture and other activities, but it is at mealtime that we gather most. Often we simply gather potluck-style in one of our homes, most of which are small New York City apartments, yet quite likely close to the size of the homes in which the first-century communities gathered. Sometimes there are only seven or so of us gathered; at other times there are a few dozen, and we are pouring out into various rooms, the front courtyard, backyard, and upstairs to other apartments. A couple times per month, we gather for a meal at the residential housing and community center on our block that supports people with issues related to addiction or mental health, and others who need various supports.

These gatherings are far from religious, although we do often pray for the meal (although sometimes not until halfway through the meal or thereafter, since folks arrive at various times). We occasionally will sing a song, but those occasions are few and far between. And only on occasion will we include a teaching. By freeing ourselves from religious trappings, we have discovered that the Spirit moves through our conversations; and often simply by being present to one another, we discover a richness of experience. Our gatherings are attended by an incredibly wide range of people, ranging from a university professor to a homeless cross-dresser, some immigrants (documented and undocumented) and some native-born, and everyone in the middle.

We often use our projector to show movies on the block during the summer or inside the community center during inclement weather. We call these showings Family Fun Night. At one point one fall, we were showing "The Princess and the Frog." There were many families present for the showing. As the community center is in the supportive housing (serving people with histories of homelessness, mental illness, and substance abuse issues), located at the end of our block, many of the residents were present as well. It was a good movie, we had pizza and snacks, and everyone was enjoying themselves.

As we were all laughing together, the director of the facility asked to speak to me privately. She told me that one of the residents had died in his room, and the ambulance was there to remove the body. I did not do as Paul in Troas and say, "Do not be alarmed!" Neither did I attempt to resurrect this person. Why would I? I had not bored him to death, as had Paul. In fact, he was not even part of our gathering that evening. What I did do was move the movie screen so that the families (and especially the children) were not facing the body bag as it was wheeled out. The adults aware of what was happening became somber, yet the children, oblivious, continued to laugh at the movie and eat pizza. After that event, we continued to regularly show movies, but we decided to change the name from Family Fun Night to Movie Night.

Christians are called to take risks. We are called to serve and preach the Gospel to the poor and oppressed, but it is more than that. We are also called to share our lives together, to watch movies and share buckets of popcorn together, to allow walls to come down, and to allow real relationships to develop. We must resist the idea that we are merely to serve and advocate for those on the margins, and enter into genuine relationships with those too often deemed *other.* That *otherness* fades away when real relationship happens.

More Models of Resistance

The Scriptures are filled with examples of minority groups resisting dominant cultures. Daniel is one such exemplar of resistance. He was born into captivity, a child of Israel's elite who had been taken into exile by Babylon, and he was considered among the most gifted of the children in exile and thus was placed in a program to educate him to serve the empire. Like Native American children who were placed in Indian Mission Schools, Daniel and his peers were removed from their families, given new names that reflected proper Babylonian culture, and forced to assimilate.

Yet, like many Native Americans, Daniel resisted the impulse to assimilate. He did not eat the food of the empire, but maintained a Jewish diet, and as a result his skin had sheen and he became heartier than those who ate the empire's delicacies. Daniel also refused King Darius' decree that no one was permitted to pray to or worship any god but Darius. Daniel's refusal caused him to be thrown into the lion's den. Even in the midst of his persecution, God was with him. The more he resisted the empire, the more he was shown favor by God and the king, and those who persecuted him in turn suffered execution; in fact, the administrators who accused Daniel and their entire families suffered death. And Darius even declared "that in all my royal dominion people should tremble and fear before the God of Daniel" (Dan. 6:26).

Some biblical scholars argue that the Book of Daniel is not historical, but that the purpose of the story was to show how Jews should live in the diaspora. It proved that Jews who remain faithful and resist assimilation will thrive despite the forces opposing them. Regardless of the historicity of Daniel, the theme of resistance remains strong in the biblical narrative.

So, who or what is it that we are resisting? James, the half-brother of Jesus, writes in his epistle that we are to *submit to God, and resist the devil* (James 4:7). We must resist all that seeks to put itself before God in our lives, such as the desire for wealth and reputation, or the desire to obtain the things of this world. Jesus tells us clearly that we are to seek first the Kingdom of God and his righteousness, and then all these *things* will be added. Yet there is a great risk that these *things* may be different when we prioritize our life to follow Christ. If not submitted to God, then another spirit or force will take authority in our lives. If held captive, we must put our hope in Jesus, call upon his name and be saved. The Word says that *the gates of hell shall not prevail*. Gates are a defensive strategy. Heaven is breaking in; it is breaking even into hell. The great Liberator, Jesus Christ, has come to set us free. He has come to heal and restore and equip us that we may help usher in the Kingdom of God.

Assimilating Jesus

Too often people make God into their own image, rather than understanding that we are made in God's image. Making God in our image becomes increasingly problematic when the dominant culture does this. In the United States, the church has turned the Near Eastern Jewish peasant we call Jesus into a white person, clearly of European descent, with sandy blonde hair and blue eyes. In this regard, they have deified white American men. And then when those from minority communities try such a thing (such as Vine Deloria, a Native American theologian, who wrote "God is Red," or James Cone, who declares over and over again in his books and lectures that God is black, or more controversially, as some LGBT theologians posit, God is gay), the dominant culture cries heresy. There is power in images and identities. There is danger when the dominant culture deifies itself, and people in the dominant culture feel threatened when a minority culture attempts to do the same. I am not advocating that Christians become aniconic but that we continually assess how we appropriate the image of God.

I learned much about contextualization from a series of murals that covered the walls of the ground floor of New York's YMPJ, where I once served as development director. YMPJ is located across from the Bronx River Housing Projects (the birthplace of hip hop) in the South Bronx in the poorest congressional district in the United States. YMPJ is a youth organization that equips young people to identify issues that affect their communities, such as the school-to-prison pipeline and environmental injustices, and organize to address those issues. The ground floor of YMPJ is called Grace Place. It is where young people, as well as staff, meet for reflection. On the walls are murals, painted by Chilean graffiti artist Nelson Rivas (aka "Cekis"), of the life of Christ in the context of the South Bronx.

In all the murals, Jesus appears Afro-Latino, occasionally with cornrows and always with kinky hair. On one wall, Jesus is being baptized in the Bronx River. In another, he is delivering the Sermon on the Mount from a fire escape on a building. Next, he is being arrested by the New York Police Department; the passage next to it reads, "He was led away by the authorities." Then Jesus is found on a table getting prepped for execution by lethal injection. Finally,

Jesus's face is shown as a mural on the side of a building where flowers and candles are left in remembrance.

Grace Place is a sacred place because of the people who meet there. The murals accurately reflect the life of Christ, yet it is done in a way that residents in the South Bronx can connect with. Jesus is made real in that space. The murals provide inspiration and challenge to live the Gospel in this world and not merely allow Christianity to be a spiritual thing with no teeth.

In my recent work at The Bowery Mission, I have been given the privilege to help decide what mural will be painted in the basement where clothes are distributed and showers are provided for the homeless community. Inspired by the murals in Grace Place, I have suggested that we contextualize the verses that we have had painted on those walls for several years: "I was hungry and you gave me food, I was a stranger and you welcomed me, I was naked and you clothed me, I was sick and you visited me." In one mural, Jesus will be receiving a meal in the dining hall of the Mission; in another he will be receiving medical services in our clinic; and lastly, he will be receiving a fresh change of clothes from the Mission's clothing room. By reflecting Jesus' vulnerability and likeness to the homeless men we serve at the Mission, they may be reminded of their eternal worth and of their likeness to God.

I preach often at the Mission, sometimes twice a day, and in my preaching I find that providing context for the community is invaluable. There is power in explaining that Mary was an unwed teenage mother, that Jesus suffered a state-sanctioned execution, and that the Holy Family was from a region oppressed by a foreign empire.

When Nathaniel, who would later become an apostle, learned that the Messiah came from Nazareth, he asked, "Can anything good come out of Nazareth?" Sometimes I will ask the community to whom I minister, "Can anything good come from the poor, from undocumented immigrants, from the drug addicted? Can anything good come from those who live in the housing projects or shelter system? Can anything good come from single moms or ex-cons?" The answer is always a resounding yes. If God came into this world through an unwed teenage mother from a bad neighborhood, if he spent his first night as an infant sleeping on straw and his last hours of life hanging on a cross, if the savior of the world suffered such challenging and tragic circumstances, then so too can each of us welcome the embrace of promise and hope, that goodness can come from us as well, regardless of where we come from or our present situation. If Jesus lived among the poor and oppressed in the first century, we might ask if it is among the poor and oppressed of the twenty-first century that we might find Jesus today.

Pursuing Holiness

Christians are called to have joy in Christ, but we are not to make happiness our goal. Joy is a deep experience that provides sustenance to our inward being, whereas happiness is a fleeting, outward expression. The framers of the Declaration of Independence knew that all they could offer others was the *right to pursue happiness*. The Declaration of Independence states that each person has the right to "Life, Liberty and the Pursuit of Happiness." Happiness is fleeting, and a fleeting emotion should not be the goal of our spiritual journey. That said, neither should joy, albeit a deeper expression, be the goal of our spiritual journey. In New York City there are subway ads from a philosophy school that claim by taking classes at this school, you will find the way to permanent happiness. But there are times when we do not, and should not, desire to be happy—the death of a loved one, or losing a job.

We are not called simply to be happy. The cherubim and seraphim were not crying "Happy, Happy is the Lord," but "Holy, Holy, Holy!" God does not say, "Be happy for I am happy." He says, "Be holy for I am holy." Sadly, most people prefer a happy God to a holy God. The concept of *holiness* is too often a loaded term. It comes with baggage and preconceived notions. Many think it means that one must spend hours in deep prayer and talk about God all the time or be an incredibly pious person. While prayer, spiritual conversation, and piety are important, holiness is more about right relationship and wholeness in one's personhood. Holiness is right relationship with God, one's neighbors, one's possessions, and creation. Holiness and righteousness are closely related. And to be holy is to be in righteous, Christ-centered relationship. This is what we are called to. We are called to be whole people in right and healthy relationships.

To journey toward holiness we must attempt to answer the enigmatic question, "What is the meaning of life?" At bookstores and libraries, shelves are filled with books attempting to answer this question. Yet Jesus speaks plainly the answer to this question when a religious scholar asked him, "What is the greatest commandment?" Jesus replies, "'You shall love the Lord your God with all your heart, and with all your soul, and with all your mind.' This is the greatest and first commandment. And a second is like it: 'You shall love your neighbor as yourself.' On these two commandments hang all the law and the prophets." Love is the answer. Love God and love others as yourself. There is almost a third commandment hidden here, as Jesus says, "love your neighbor as yourself." We are called to love ourselves as well. This is not a self-centered love, but an acknowledgment that we are *lovable*, that God loves us, and we should love that which God loves, which includes ourselves. The Scriptures declare that "God is love." Thus this is the meaning of life: to love radically, deeply, and with abandon. To love, not so much in a mushy, sentimental way, but in a deep, substantive way that allows God to enter into all of our relationships.

Chapter 7

Revolution as Ongoing Act

For whenever I speak, I must cry out,
    I must shout, "Violence and destruction!"
For the word of the Lord has become for me
    a reproach and derision all day long.
If I say, "I will not mention him,
    or speak any more in his name,"
then within me there is something like a burning fire
    shut up in my bones;
I am weary with holding it in,
    and I cannot.

—Jeremiah 20:8–9

Revelation reveals the truth . . . It takes a revolution to make a solution.

—Bob Marley

There is an unsavory relationship between politics and religion in the United States. This is especially noticeable in the midst of election seasons, when all the political and religious peacocks have their feathers flared in an effort to draw the attention of voters toward their particular agendas. However, the rhetoric and ideologues persist even when there is no election. Many who call themselves Christians continue to condemn rather than lift up those whom they perceive as *sinners*. Paul wrote to the church in Corinth that we are not to judge those outside the church but are called to judge those inside. "For what have I to do with judging those outside? Is it not those who are inside that you are to judge? God will judge those outside. Drive out the wicked person from among you" (1 Cor. 5:12–13). We are called to suffer for those outside the church and lay down our lives as Christ did for us so that they too might encounter God's redemptive power.

Christians are citizens of the Kingdom of God and thus subject to the Most High. We are, in a sense, representatives, or ambassadors, of the coming Kingdom. We are here for only a season, and we are supposed to obey the laws of the land just as we would obey the laws of any country in which we are a visitor. And, regardless of a nation's laws, we must remain faithful to God and, even if, or perhaps especially if, we suffer or struggle due to unjust laws, we must pray for the heads of nations just like Paul did in prison and Christ did on the cross. A follower of Christ must believe that prayer is more powerful than protest marches. It is through prayer that God is invited into the situation and through God's presence the protest is given power.

Too often Christians employ politics rather than prayer and godly love as a medium to express their hopes. Thus they become inevitably yoked to a doomed system. We, as Christians, need to think outside politics. In the Book of Acts, the Christians were often persecuted; Peter and John are arrested (Acts 4:3–22), Stephen (Acts 6:8–8:1) had just been martyred, and Paul and his co-laborers are routinely chased out of towns (Acts 17:1–15). They could have used a political or marketing campaign to change the tide of politics. They could have argued to the Roman government that one more *god* (Jesus) would not hurt their pantheon of deities. But they chose to pray. And when they prayed, the gates of the prison were opened and Peter was freed. Christians must pray and love one another to thus further establish the Kingdom of God.

This world, polluted by corrupt systems and our own separation from God, encourages arrogance, sexual immorality, and contention. Vanity is emulated in the media and blasphemy is considered a common part of the English vernacular. God's commandments are stricter than the world's social norms. John writes that if you curse your brother, you are a murderer (1 John 3:15). Jesus says in the Sermon on the Mount that if you lust after a woman who is not your wife, you have already committed adultery in your heart. In the same chapter Jesus commands, "Love your enemies and pray for those who persecute you, so that you may be children of your Father in heaven" (Matt. 5:44–45). This is a far cry from cursing others and judging those lost in sin.

Like Christ, we must chastise the religious hypocrites, false prophets, and those who cause division in the body of believers. Like Christ, we must love those separated from God so that they too might encounter God's loving embrace. We are not called to be political provocateurs. We are not called to spread democracy, socialism, or any other type of worldly government. Christians are called to establish further the Kingdom of God by allowing Christ to love others through them. Instead of voting to criminalize unwed mothers who are considering abortion, we are called to love them, even bleed for them. Instead of cursing gay marriage, Christians should work to sanctify their own marriages. Instead of donating money to right-wing or left-wing political causes, Christians can invest personally in the lives of those they want to affect. They can volunteer at a rescue mission on a regular basis or extend hospitality to a person in need. We are called to pray for peace in Jerusalem but also to pray for peace in Beirut, Kabul, and Pyongyang.

Christians need to stop calling themselves conservative or liberal, and take up the radical charge Christ has given us. Christ was not a conservative. It was the conservative establishment that crucified him. He was, in actuality, a radical, a real revolutionary. When Jesus began his ministry, he did not seek approval of the Sadducees or Pharisees or Essenes or any other religious order. He went to the most extreme religious figure of his day, John the Baptizer, and received his baptism from him. As citizens of the Kingdom of God, we must abide by the radical laws that God has ordered us to follow. Christ said to love God with all your heart and to love your neighbor as yourself (Matt. 22:36–39). If we really obeyed these commandments, we would see revival not only in our churches, but also in our neighborhoods and across nations.

With regard to worldly politics, I am unable to find Christ's agenda in Scripture. In fact, his only agenda was to bleed for others. Simon the Zealot (who, it is assumed because of his title, was part of a guerilla terrorist group that tried to reclaim Israel by force) and Matthew (a tax collector and pawn of the Roman state) were both Christ's apostles. They came from complete opposite ends of the political spectrum. In fact, the Zealots sometimes assassinated tax collectors to make a political statement. But Christ called them both to be his disciples. Their political differences are never mentioned in Scripture.

Compared to the politically tumultuous time in which Christ lived, Americans, even in the aftermath of 9/11 and the economic turmoil of 2008, live in relative peace and prosperity. The two dominant American political parties have similar agendas: protection of national security, the free market, and individual rights. During the life of Christ, Israel was in a state of complete cultural upheaval. Within the Jewish community in Israel there were several factions that opposed one another politically and religiously, often violently. Among the many factions were Pharisees (a priestly, more democratic class), Sadducees (a priestly, wealthy aristocracy that collaborated with Rome, and controlled the temple), Zealots (a violent insurgent group bent on Israel's independence), and Essenes (desert dwellers awaiting the imminent arrival of the Messiah), and within these factions there was even greater division. Amidst this intense political background, Christ did not align himself with any factions but made a new way.

Many (including some of Jesus' own disciples) believed that the Messiah would come bearing the sword. They did not understand that the Kingdom of God extended beyond political boundaries. Christ did not come to solve the political problems of the world. If he had come for political power, he would have succumbed to Satan's temptation in the desert. That is, he would have worshiped Satan in exchange for authority over all the kingdoms of the world. But Christ did not come to take over worldly governments. He came to establish the Kingdom of God. Whenever a person tried to corner Jesus into answering a contentious political question, he responded with an answer straight from his Kingdom.

In Luke, some of Jesus's opponents among the Pharisees sent people in an attempt to dupe Jesus into saying something that would provide a pretext for his arrest. The Pharisees believed it was idolatrous to use a Roman coin because on it was Caesar's image (it also had on it the inscription "Divus," which means "god"). The conspirators asked Jesus, "Is it lawful for us to pay taxes to the emperor, or not?"

Jesus asked them to pull out a coin and then asked, "Whose head and whose title does it bear?" They replied that it had the emperor's image on it. Christ said, "Then give to the emperor the things that are the emperor's, and to God the things that are God's." He could have given an easy answer (either "Yes, pay your taxes," or "No, do not pay your taxes"), but he chose to respond to a politically motivated question with a radical, godly answer. Jesus Christ is commanding that we submit our whole selves to God since we are made in God's image. Christ's Kingdom is not of this world, so his commandments seem foreign to those whose eyes are closed to the Gospel. While worldly governments employ violence (military, police) to control the people, Christ commanded us to love and suffer for others so that his Kingdom will be further established.

I am not advocating that Christians should disobey their government in every situation. Paul writes to the Romans, "Let every person be subject to the governing authorities; for there is no authority except from God" (Rom. 13:1). I am saying that if we call ourselves Christians, then we must be like Christ. That does not mean we should be like Old Testament judges or even like the faithful centurion in the New Testament. It means that we must be like Christ. He commands us to be "wise as serpents and innocent as doves."

Whereas governments mobilize armies to defeat their enemies, Christ rescued the poor and oppressed, healed the diseased and demon-possessed by the power of the Holy Spirit, and suffered on the cross so that we might be saved. Christ never commanded his followers to organize politically, take up arms, rail at sexual minorities, or curse unwed mothers, but that is what many who call themselves Christians have chosen to do. The body of Christ is being co-opted, infected by politics and greed. Politically motivated Christians are busy patting themselves on the back for being good citizens while Christianity is being perceived as an increasingly hostile and judgmental religion. Sinners ran to Jesus, but people are running from the church (which is supposed to be Christ's body). People are afraid they will be judged in church rather than saved. Prostitutes, tax collectors, and other sinners were attracted to Jesus, but today many parishioners would rather keep the *filth* out of the church than to let them enter in and be washed by the blood.

In John 8, some of Jesus's opponents among the Pharisees tried to trap Jesus into speaking against the Law of Moses. They brought him a woman caught in the act of adultery and asked, "Now in the law Moses commanded us to stone such women. Now what do you say?" Jesus, drawing in the dust, said, "Let anyone among you who is without sin be the first to throw a stone at her." The Pharisees left, being convicted by their own conscience. Jesus looked up and asked the woman where her accusers had gone. She told him they had left. He then said to her, "Neither do I condemn you. Go your way, and from now on do not sin again."

What these Pharisees failed to understand is that Christ came not to condemn, but to save those who are lost, outcast, and accused. Christians who have never held the hand of a woman considering abortion, but are quick to vote to criminalize these troubled women, should repent because they have just taken sides with the stone-throwing mob of Pharisees rather than with Jesus.

Many politically motivated evangelists (and their followers alike) have tried to use the law to justify their own supposed morality, which is founded not in God, but in their own will. They are trying to mobilize Christians around issues rather than encouraging believers to bleed for people. These so-called evangelists have made a second, inferior image of the body of Christ, and that image is deceiving the mass of people who need salvation. Christians need to have mercy on the unsaved as Christ had mercy on us. Christians need to start living more like Christ than like a Pharisee, a Roman, or an American. We need to identify with Christ before even considering our national, ethnic, or economic identity. We need to ask ourselves if we are quicker to bleed for others or quicker to throw stones.

Revelation as Revolution

John the Revelator was exiled to Mount Athos by the Roman politicos who sought to silence his prophetic voice. But it was in exile that God spoke through him with greatest clarity. John's Revelation includes seven letters to seven churches, and a scathing rebuke and renunciation of the powers and principalities of this world. The first three chapters consist of John's letters to the seven faith communities. These letters include dense characterizations of the early churches, especially evident is the diversity of these communities and the conflicts they face.

John's Revelation is a declaration of war. It explicitly describes the war between Babylon (that is, Rome and/or cultures of domination) and God. In particular, John is addressing the abuses of the Roman Empire, yet he never mentions Rome by name; his proclamation in many respects is universal, a rebuke and renunciation of all systems of domination and oppression. Although Rome is never named, John provides ample evidence that his rebuke is directed at this great city that he refers to as Babylon the Great Whore. In Revelation 17:9, John refers to the "seven mountains" on which the "Great Whore" sits. Rome is situated on seven hills, and it is from that seat of power that Rome/Babylon exerts its domination over other territories.

Much of the rest of Revelation addresses Rome's state-sponsored terrorism in the first century. The first Jewish temple was destroyed by Babylon in 586 BCE, and Rome destroyed the second temple in 70 CE. Rome not only conquered and occupied other territories, but also intimidated other countries to become part of the empire. Rome was known for its military strength, its relationship with client-kings, and its commerce. The angel reveals through John: "Come, I will show you the judgment of the great whore who is seated on many waters, with whom the kings of the earth have committed fornication, and with the wine of whose fornication the inhabitants of the earth have become drunk" (Rev. 17:1–2). According to John, these kings have whored themselves out to Babylon. They have made deals in an attempt to secure their interests and power. Revelation describes the woman who sits upon the beast, the woman who may be the great whore herself, as "full of blasphemous names" (Rev. 17:3). This may very well be a reference to Caesar, who applied divine names to himself. John also rebukes the merchants and politicians who weep when their wealth and trade routes are destroyed (Rev. 17, 18).

In our time, American Christians (who wield unprecedented power) have used Scriptures to justify slavery and lynching, exploitative capitalism, mass incarceration, and other social evils. Whereas peasants and urban poor suffered state-sponsored terror and oppression in the Roman Empire, so too have many in the United States suffered state-sponsored racial terrorism often at the hands of wealthy white Christians. Many have suffered social marginalization due to poverty and lack of access to resources and wealth, under-education and limited skills, and immigration status.

The church is a living, breathing body. It does change and take new forms. We see in the first century that many Christians are experimenting with various models of shared housing, dinner churches, and other forms of worship and gathering. Today, the institutional church is in decline, but new creative forms of sharing life in Christ are emerging.

Liberation before Transformation

In Numbers 13:26–14:4, we learn that the Hebrew people have escaped the bondage of Egypt. They were delivered from the slavery and the oppression placed upon them by the dominant culture. They witnessed miracles and God's provision. And now they were headed to the land that God promised them. Moses, the leader of this liberation movement, sent scouts, including Joshua and Caleb, to investigate the land God was giving them. It truly was a land flowing with milk and honey, but there were enemies in the land, giants and fortified cities, obstacles to overcome before they could enter into the promise God had for them. The spies returned with the report, and the people were fearful rather than faithful. Only Joshua and Caleb had faith to enter God's promise for them; they knew God was with them. But the people wept over their children, afraid they would be killed, and wives and children taken as plunder. They forgot how God had delivered them from Egypt. They still had an enslavement mentality, still numb from the generational suffering they endured in Egypt—out of Egypt but still, in some ways, captive.

The people wanted to believe the promise was for them, that they were stronger than giants, and had the tactical expertise to overcome fortified cities. They wanted to believe that their God *is* God and would guide them, but they were still working out their liberation. They had risen up against Egypt and pursued their freedom, yet even beyond Egypt's borders they were struggling to understand what it means to be free. To be a changed person, to be a new person, is to be a person with agency, free to make choices, and free to trust God's Word, regardless of the dominant culture's resistance to the liberating truth of that word.

Liberation is a precondition to transformation. Before one can actually change one's life situation, one needs to be free to do so. Once we are liberated, we begin to have a change of mind and heart and lifestyle. Our eyes begin to open. We begin to have deeper knowledge and understanding of who we are and who we are called to be. We are no longer a slave to the old way. We begin to find our freedom in Christ, and never again will anyone be able to place a harness upon us. We need to live into that freedom, into that hope and that promise that God has for each and every one of us.

Too often people in this world, people in the church, have this mental and spiritual enslavement. They have yet to be changed because they have yet to be free. People may think they are free because they are not behind bars, not in physical bondage, but the mind and spirit is still captive. There are many today who are slaves to a cruel master—whether it is unhealthy relationships, consumerism, alcohol and drugs, arrogance, ignorance, or unforgiveness.

Soon after the Hebrews escaped Egypt, shortly after Miriam sang her song of deliverance with timbrel in hand, with all the women dancing and all the people following them through the Red Sea, almost as soon as the people were out of Egypt, they began to murmur and express their desire to return to the culture that despised and used them. In one moment they are singing God's praises and his power to overturn their captors:

> Sing to the Lord, for he has triumphed gloriously;
> horse and rider he has thrown into the sea.
> (Exod. 15:21)

The next moment, during times of trial and tribulation, they desire death in captivity and dream of life in a world that hated them: "If only we had died by the hand of the Lord in the land of Egypt, when we sat by the fleshpots and ate our fill of bread; for you have brought us out into this wilderness to kill this whole assembly with hunger" (Exod. 16:3).

Yet is this not all of us? Sometimes we fail to see how far we have come, especially when we still have so far to go. We also must work out our liberation. Too often we want to run back to that which had once enslaved us because it comforts us, provides us with a sense of familiarity, or some other false reason.

There is a certain comfort, or numbness, in mental enslavement. You do not have to think or try or do anything besides accept the situation you are in. And we can be like the Israelites and grumble and murmur and simply accept despair and spiritual poverty. We may not be in physical bondage, but many of us still lack the freedom to live the way God wants us to live. The liberation that leads toward transformation begins with choices and changes we need to make that we may be positioned to enter the promise when God calls. But sometimes we have been ingrained with lies for so long that we begin to believe the lies told about us and others.

The Scriptures explain that there are systems, principalities, and powers that seek to dominate and destroy us. The world tries to keep whole people groups down, to keep people in their place. Political pundits and the media manipulate ideas and culture in order to maintain the status quo. Some years ago, I had the privilege to meet and attend a church dinner with Dick Gregory, the civil rights activist, comedian, nutritionist, and one-time presidential candidate. He was speaking at Nazarene Congregation UCC in Bedford-Stuyvesant about black-on-black hate crimes. This is a term popularly used by media and pundits. It has been absorbed into the culture and accepted without critique by the majority of people. Mr. Gregory challenged this pervasive notion. He noted that somehow we believe that when a black person commits a crime, it is more hateful. But how, he asked, is one ethnicity's crimes more hateful than another's? And he reminded us that people commit crimes most often where they live. Black people commit crimes in black neighborhoods, Hasidic people commit crimes in Hasidic neighborhoods, and Chinese people commit crimes in Chinese neighborhoods.

Liberation theologians, particularly James Cone, employ the exodus narrative as a parallel to the African American experience. From enslavement to emancipation, and the struggle for personal and cultural transformation, the experience of Africans in America shares similar themes with the Hebrews in Egypt. Thus some liberationists are critical of the desire of many European Americans for racial reconciliation. Cone, in particular, slows down the white liberal desire for racial reconciliation. Many white progressives desire racial reconciliation but have failed to recognize, as Cone posits, that their foot is still firmly planted on the neck of the oppressed. The Israelites who escaped bondage in Egypt did not seek reconciliation with their captors; they sought liberation. For those who suffer under discriminatory policies and are the target of racist laws, Egypt is still the reality.

The story in Numbers (and Exodus) continues. The generation that wept over their babies, who feared their wives and children would be taken as plunder, had to pass away before the next generation could enter into the promise. We can live like the Israelites who had fear and wandered in the wilderness for forty years, or we can have faith that the Holy One will see us through. We need faith. God spoke through James, brother of Jesus, that if we do not have faith, we should ask God for it, who gives abundantly. James also wrote that we should ask for wisdom, and the Lord will pour out wisdom upon us because he does not want us to live that old way anymore. We need faith and wisdom if we are to break through, if we are to enter into God's promise for us.

All of us, starting with me, are in some kind of bondage. None of us are fully redeemed and Christ-like just yet. So those of us who think we have it all together need to go to the Lord and ask where we need to grow or where we are holding back from God. But I think that most of us know where we struggle. Sometimes we just need to spend time in the wilderness to work out our faith.

The ultimate expression of liberation is in the resurrection as a symbol of newness, transformation, and change. This is how we need to live. Some people live in another way: they talk about standing on the promises of God, declaring how God will expand *their* territories, and so on. But we must read these passages from Scripture in context.

There are other promises that God has for us: that we will have to carry our cross, that we will be persecuted and endure suffering. Another promise is that we will have to die to ourselves. The old person has to die so that the new person might live. This is the power of the resurrection. This is the newness into which we need to live. We all need to be liberated, to be set free.

Chapter 8

Radical Praxis

For apart from inquiry, apart from the praxis, individuals cannot be truly human. Knowledge emerges only through invention and re-invention, through the restless, impatient, continuing, hopeful inquiry human beings pursue in the world, with the world, and with each other.

—Paulo Freire, *Pedagogy of the Oppressed*

Liberationists from Gustavo Gutierrez to James Cone articulate a theology that deemphasizes the primary importance of theology and thus emphasizes the necessity of praxis as the first act of the Christian life. Throughout his work, Gutierrez explains that theology must be the second act. Praxis comes first and then theological reflection. Since a very young age, I have felt called to write my thoughts, either through prose or poetry. And while I made a living throughout my twenties as a reporter, writer, and research editor, I was not prepared to reflect upon my spiritual experiences for a larger audience because I was still deeply immersed in exploring what my experience meant for me. I was not yet able to articulate the personal and social implications of my experience with others seeking and occasionally encountering the Most High. Although I am still immersed in the journey, it is after nearly ten years of living in community that I feel prepared to begin a genuine reflection on praxis. One must live their faith before they can attempt to truly explain it.

James, the half-brother of Jesus, writes in his epistle:

> What good is it, my brothers and sisters, if you say you have faith but do not have works? Can faith save you? If a brother or sister is naked and lacks daily food, and one of you says to them, "Go in peace; keep warm and eat your fill," and yet you do not supply their bodily needs, what is the good of that? So faith by itself, if it has no works, is dead.
>
> But someone will say, "You have faith and I have works." Show me your faith apart from your works, and I by my works will show you my faith. (James 2:14–18)

When we replace the words "faith" with "theology" and "works" with "praxis" we begin to get a grasp of the importance of an integrated Christian life. *What good is it if someone claims to have theology but has no praxis?* This is not to argue that these texts should be translated in this way by any means but simply that the concepts, in a basic way, are related. Our faith moves us beyond ourselves. What does it matter if someone has a developed systematic theology and yet remains removed from those whom Christ not only calls us to love, but calls us to share our life with? What does it matter if someone grasps the key doctrines of the faith but does not have Christ's love for the poor and oppressed?

Praxis is not merely the practice or outward action of the faith. It far surpasses mere deeds or acts of service. Praxis is a holistic expression of faith that integrates all elements, personal and social, into the life of the disciple and demonstrates that integrated faith as the inward-outward tension of the Christian witness.

The Christian life begins with an encounter with God that leads to transformation. Jesus' first miracle occurred during the wedding at Cana. The wedding party had run out of wine, and Jesus' mother encouraged her son to help. After some prompting, Jesus told the servants to fill with water the six large cisterns used for ceremonial washing. The jars were used to hold water for purification rites such as washing hands and the outer body before prayer and offering sacrifice. Religious adherents connected outer cleanliness with inner purity. During this first miracle, Jesus signaled how his ministry was different from the dominant religion of his time. He turned the *holy* water into incredibly good wine. Upon tasting the wine, the master of the banquet proclaimed, "You have saved the best till now." Throughout the Scriptures, wine is a symbol of the Holy Spirit. Instead of washing the outer body with water, Jesus turns the water to wine that then enters the inside of the person. Jesus was concerned with cleaning the "outer cup as well as the inner cup." It is through this wine, this Spirit that enters us, changes us, intoxicates us with the divine, that we are transformed and seek to live out our faith, to enter into new relationships, and serve a Holy God that loves us and seeks to manifest his love through us.

Praxis involves the participation in right relationship with God, one's self, and others. It implies genuine participation in the life of Christ, a life aimed at ministry to and with the poor, blind, imprisoned, and oppressed.

Praxis of Presence

Following Christ draws us into relationships with people we would have previously sought to exploit, ignore, or marginalize. It draws us closer to people we may have wanted to kill, literally or figuratively. As mentioned in the previous chapter, two of Jesus' apostles were dramatically opposed to one another, Simon the Zealot and Matthew the tax collector. Zealots were a guerilla terrorist group whose aim was to overturn Rome's stronghold on Israel and thus restore Israel as an independent nation. Tax collectors were locals who represented the interests of the empire. Often zealots assassinated tax collectors. Yet, in Christ, the two, Simon the Zealot and Matthew the tax collector, turned from their previous vocations to become disciples of Jesus of Nazareth. Relationship with God through Christ has the power to transform relationships in this world.

At The Bowery Mission, we have a weekly Bible study. It is mostly comprised of ten to thirty men and women who are either chronically homeless or housing-insecure. The group changes each week, but there is a core group that has been part of the Bible study for a couple of years. On occasion, I invite volunteer groups who serve at the Mission for a week or so to join our weekly Bible study. I have had several ministers tell me that their participation in the Bible study was the most transformative part of their mission trip. Usually the volunteer experience consists of serving meals, distributing clothes, and leading chapel services. The volunteers are always giving, always in a position of power and privilege. That changes in the Bible study, where the hierarchy of volunteer and homeless person fades away. Everyone is on the same ground. All are eating from the same basket of cookies and drinking from the same pot of coffee.

Each Bible study begins with an icebreaker question that is framed positively and attempts to bring hope or good remembrance to mind. During one Bible study the icebreaker question was "Where did you go to feel safe when you were a child?" On that particular day, we had about fifteen members of the homeless community, and we were visited by an affluent church group's youth ministry from Boston. There is one dear brother named Frank who has been part of the study since its inception. Responding to the icebreaker, Frank explained how he grew up in the South Bronx during the 1970s during a time of intense poverty and planned shrinkage, and when arson ravaged many neighborhoods. Many property owners burned their buildings for the insurance claims, and people stripped copper and other valuable materials from buildings. Much of the South Bronx burned. Frank explained that as a little boy he went into these burned-out buildings and cleaned out rooms and whole floors. It was in these burned-out buildings that Frank found his *safe place* as a child.

After Frank shared, the teenage girl from the youth group sitting next to him shared. She said that she is still a child since she is a teenager and then explained that her family has a second home on the harbor where they also have a yacht. And in her family's yacht, there is a small room that she uses as her safe place. She did not explain further about her safe place but simply shared and passed to the next person.

The unintentional yet seemingly divinely ordained juxtaposition of these two people's stories spoke volumes to our small Bible study. The idea of what is *safe* varies according to one's perspective. Most parents would not allow their child to play in burned-out buildings, and most children would not find such places to be *safe*, which leads one to question Frank's home life as a child. What happened in his home to drive him into a burned-out building for safety? We live in a broken world, and seldom will we notice the severity of that brokenness until we meet others in situations of extreme scarcity and abuse as well as those in abundance and privilege. When we hear each other's stories, we humanize one another. Biases and stereotypes fade away, and we become real to one another. It is through these encounters, by simply being present to one another and listening to each other's stories, do ideologies and opinions regarding race, class, and more, which are often formed by media or other sources, begin to change. Encountering one another in the Spirit of Christ transforms perspective and grants understanding.

There are many ways that the powers and principalities seek to undermine and subvert this work that leads to transformation of the individual as well as the society. Thus we must remain guarded and persevere in working out our liberation. In my work at The Bowery Mission, I see many good-hearted people every day who donate money, food, and clothes. Many also donate their time by volunteering in the kitchen or other places. This charity greatly helps the Mission continue its important work, yet it is when volunteers regularly visit the Mission, share meals with the community, and participate in the Bible study as equals, without the trappings of merely offering a handout, that we see changed minds, hearts, and perceptions. Volunteers become peers with members of the community, and occasionally they become friends.

Lila Watson, an Aboriginal Australian activist, once told a group of European Australian women who wanted to donate to her cause, "If you have come here to give me charity, no thanks. If you've come here because your liberation is tied up with ours, then let's work together." We are all knit together. Our liberation, our salvation is tied together. If one of us suffers, all of us suffer. If one of us is in bondage, we are all in bondage. Awakening to this reality and choosing to turn from accepting the present social structure and working toward creating another world is the first step in genuine repentance.

Work as Praxis

Radical Living is a community where people have the opportunity to experiment with their faith. It is a place to be supported and strengthened by others, and a place to support and strengthen others. Each of our individual journeys and our personal relationship with God is interwoven with our service to the coming Kingdom. In community, we attempt to balance the tension of inward reflection and piety and outward service and action. Faith has deeply affected the vocations of many who live in Radical Living. From bridge engineer to bike messenger, members of Radical Living have sought to find purpose in their work.

The faith community, or church, is the place to equip and encourage the saints. It is from the faith community that the people go out to share God's light and love with the world. For example, we currently have three members who are social workers. They are committed to counsel, support, and help heal those who are hurting. One member is concerned about the environment and the food we consume. In her vocation, she manages several green markets. Another member is a dual-language school teacher in East New York. And yet another is a bridge engineer and, although he struggled for a while to understand how his work is a service to God, he has expressed that he gets great joy from engineering and knows that it is his calling. Similarly, my wife's work is to engage local congregations to educate and equip them to improve their environmental practices. Although these vocations are not exclusively religious, they are rooted in a concern for others and our planet.

My work as the Director of Chapel and Compassionate Care at The Bowery Mission is the most overtly religious, yet my journey here has not been without questions or concerns. As a young man I was a furniture mover for a few years, worked in many factories, and worked four years as a seasonal track maintainer for a regional railroad company. I have had a wide range of jobs, much of them working alongside rough-and-tumble men. Looking back, these experiences prepared me to work with the men I serve at the Mission. Throughout my teens and twenties, I also spent time in and out of jail, often for only a weekend but up to three months for my actions in South Korea. These experiences prepared me for the work I now do.

Creating Holy Days

An integrated life is an outcome of a life rooted in praxis. Seeking meaning and the means to express the hope found in the Gospel in a world fraught with competition, greed, and isolation is important to the devout. Sharing life together, whether in intentional community or some other way, presents opportunities, blessings, and challenges. Having lived in community for nearly a decade, and participating in the life of Radical Living since its inception, I have had the opportunity to witness the development and formation of various practices and observances unique to our community. Two annual traditions that began during our first years include Mystery Magi and Melinda Day. These traditions are built on or spun off of other traditions, but at Radical Living they became distinct to our shared life and practices.

Mystery Magi is our Christmas celebration, although it is perhaps more accurately called in its current form our Epiphany observance. Epiphany is one of the oldest-observed Christian holidays, although currently it is held in low esteem or neglected altogether by the majority of Christians in the West. Epiphany commemorates the magi who visited the baby Jesus and provided his family the gifts of myrrh, frankincense, and gold. This holiday was popularly observed among early Christians, likely due to its celebration of the first non-Jews to recognize Christ's sovereignty (and perhaps divinity). In popularity, Epiphany even surpassed Christmas, which was actually not regularly observed until well into the fourth century. In fact, Christmas was initially part of the Epiphany observance. Christmas later became the dominant Christian holiday and seemingly replaced most other festivals and observances in the region, although not without drawing in elements of pagan traditions such as aspects of the solstice celebration and Rome's Saturnalia festival.

Mystery Magi began as a spin-off of Secret Santa. It was, more or less, a gift exchange in which the gift giver must provide three gifts just as Jesus received three gifts. The giver cannot spend more than ten dollars, and at least one gift must be handmade by the giver. The recipient of the gifts is allowed three guesses as to who their giver is. Later developments include that the giver may give the gifts in the days and weeks leading up to the celebration. Initially, the celebration was held the week or two before Christmas, but more recently the date has shifted to the weekend nearest Epiphany. The movement of Mystery Magi to a date closer to Epiphany has allowed our community to observe together an ancient Christian holiday in a contemporary context.

Melinda Day is another annual tradition we observe at Radical Living. It is named for founding (and current) member Melinda. This tradition began in Melinda's family to observe the day she was adopted, December 6. Upon moving into Radical Living, she wanted to share this tradition with the community but did not want it to be all about her. Rather she expressed that she would like it to be a day that each of us celebrates part of our culture or identity either through song, poetry, clothing, or some other such thing. The community insisted that we continue to call it Melinda Day since she was the inspiration, but the day has since grown beyond her.

Reflecting upon these Radical Living holidays, I feel as if we have been given a glimpse into how other holidays and traditions may have started and developed. My friend and professor of New Testament at Union Theological Seminary, Hal Taussig, once told me, "Wouldn't it be wonderful if Melinda Day outlasted the actual Melinda?" There is something profound in this statement in that it pushes one to consider how other ancient traditions originally began and what layered meanings have been added to these celebrations.

Many Christian holidays have pagan origins. If a holiday has pagan roots or is ahistorical, should we abandon its observance? I argue a resounding no. Each of us, individually, but also collectively, gives meaning to such things as holidays, rituals, and traditions, and even religious experience. And even if some observances have pagan origins, we have the power to redeem such festivities and holidays.

Even within the Bible, holidays developed over time. For example, Shavout (Pentecost) was initially a harvest festival. It later became the day to commemorate the giving of the Torah at Sinai. And in the New Testament, it is the day when the Holy Spirit is given to the first Christians. It is important to understand where traditions come from, that they are not stagnant, but have life, and we are an essential part of that life in that we give such observances their meanings. We give holidays and traditions their power that eventually speaks truths not only to us, but through us to others.

Each year while working at YMPJ, we organized a Stations of the Cross liturgy that addressed the issues that affect the South Bronx. Many communities across the country participate in such contemporary versions of the

Stations of the Cross. Each station is reflected upon and also related to a current issue such as mass incarceration, unjust immigration policies, and environmental injustices. Connecting ancient practices to contemporary issues enlivens the truths of the Gospel. It roots us in the first-century reality and demythologizes the too-often overly spiritualized reflections of Christ's brutal journey to the cross. Similarly, many parishes and churches (particularly in Latino neighborhoods) have Posada celebrations/liturgies at Christmastime, giving a contemporary reality to the Nativity story.

Praxis of Radical Living

Apart from recognizing the importance of praxis in one's vocation, celebrations and observances, and relationships, there are many ways that faith communities can benefit from identifying the importance of praxis in the life of the faithful. In the first year of Radical Living, the founding members realized that for our community to be part of a movement of the Spirit rather than part of a passing trend, we needed to create structures to help sustain us. We also needed to identify who we were and what was our purpose. We spent the first year of Radical Living creating a covenant with one another. This developed into a document we call the Way of Radical Living; it is inspired by the ancient monastics who kept a rule. The rule kept by monastics, *regula* in Latin, is less a set of dos and don'ts, and more a structure to guide the adherent into deeper faith. The original rule was penned by Saint Benedict in the sixth century for monks sharing life in community and has laid the foundation for all monastic communities since in the Western church.

A rule in the Benedictine sense of the word is far different from the common understanding of what a rule is in our contemporary context. Rules in this world are often a list of things not to do, such as "no running at the pool." A rule in the Benedictine sense of the word provides a means to draw the spiritual adherent into closer intimacy with God. It is a pattern for a life that is shared in Christian community. Ultimately, it is liberating and strengthening. For example, the fifty-third chapter of the Rule of Saint Benedict deals with ways that one should extend hospitality to others. It explains how courtesy and kindness should be at the heart of hospitality.

The Way of Radical Living describes our shared values, and much of it is written in the future tense as a sign of what we hope to obtain through our life together. It reads,

> The Way of Radical Living is dedicated to a meditative, prophetic and prayerful life, centered in Christ, engaged in our neighborhood, concerned with social justice, and led by the Holy Spirit. Radical Living is a multicultural, intergenerational, and ecumenical co-housing community that seeks to embody Jesus' presence, particularly in the Bedford-Stuyvesant neighborhood of Brooklyn, New York.
>
> The three foundations of Radical Living consist of communal living, community service, and prophetic action (i.e. social justice). It is our intent to center our lives in Jesus Christ, and prayerfully enter into the holy presence to discern God's will for our lives and for our community. We will submit to the authority of the Holy Scriptures, composed

of the Torah, Prophets and Writings of the Hebrew Scriptures as well as the Gospels, Acts of the Apostles and letters of the New Testament.

We will share our lives with one another meeting together often for fellowship, prayer and common meals. We will live simply and share resources. We will be accountable to one another, confessing our sins when the Spirit prompts, and loving one another with Christ's love. We will encourage one another in the fruit of the Spirit. If there is a conflict between members we will refer to Matthew 18:15–20 as our guide to resolve the issue at hand. We will speak in love, honestly and openly, to one another.

We will be present to Bedford-Stuyvesant. We will intentionally build friendships with our neighbors, local organizations and merchants, and we will remember the people of Bed-Stuy in our daily prayers. We will remain humble and know that we have much to learn from our neighbors. We will reach out and serve our neighbors in tangible ways, and actively listen to and seek to understand the concerns of our neighbors. We will share the gospel always and, as Saint Francis said, use words when necessary.

We will be a prophetic community. We will follow the path blazed by the prophets of the Holy Scriptures and speak out against injustice, especially in our neighborhood. We will be prophetic in word and deed. We will confront unjust policies and discourses that perpetuate discrimination and oppress the marginalized. We will proclaim the gospel on the streets, in the subways, and in Borough Hall.

> We will avail ourselves to the power of the gospel so that God may work through us to heal, redeem, and restore creation.

The Way of Radical Living later became part of a larger document we developed called the Praxis of Radical Living. Our Praxis describes how we attempt to live out or practice our life together in community. It is very much a living document and is regularly updated to reflect life in our community. As we have developed this document, we remain vigilant in recognizing the necessity and danger of structure, and we attempt to establish structures not as a prescription for our community but as a description of how we function. Specifically, the Praxis is a resource to help us foster a community of compassion, spiritual formation, and Kingdom-building, and to help hold us accountable to the mission and vision of Radical Living. A few structures included in the Praxis that help to guide our community include a description of our rhythm, the decision-making process, our model for conflict resolution, and our various ministries such as prayer, finance, and hospitality.

Rhythm

The *rhythm* of Radical Living consists of prayer, shared meals, and fellowship. There is a rhythm to everything. Each person, family, and community, whether intentional or not, has a certain rhythm. The purpose of our rhythm is to express our love to God, one another, and neighbors through Jesus Christ. All of our gatherings are open to neighbors, visitors, friends, and strangers, and we welcome all who would like to participate in our rhythm of community. Our rhythm changes seasonally. We also have an inward rhythm consisting of private prayer, meditation on a Gospel text, and occasional fasting. Although our community is open and inclusive, there are times when our meetings are members only, particularly when we are making collective decisions that affect our community.

Decision Making

There are many church models for *making decisions*, ranging from elder led to congregational. There are also a great variety of decision-making models in the Bible. For example, Moses and the exodus community evolved their model for making decisions (as well as for demonstrating leadership) over time. Due to the influence of Jethro, Moses' father-in-law, Moses ceased to make all the decisions for his community and appointed men "as officials over thousands, hundreds, fifties and tens." Jethro was a Midianite priest, and thus not an Israelite, yet he provided the model for effective decision making. The inspiration for Radical Living's model for decision making was initially inspired by my experience living in a co-op during college at the University of Wisconsin-Madison. Radical Living has developed our decision-making process over time, and we have found Scriptures to support various models.

In the beginning of our community, we were fairly anarchistic. Within a few months of the life of the community, we implemented consensus decision making as our process. Currently, we practice a hybrid of consensus and elder-led decision making. Various ministries within our community and several communally appointed coordinators of those ministries have been designated to exercise the power to make certain decision. For example, if there is a request for funds from the common purse, the treasurer can allocate up to $50 at her discretion, and the finance ministry can allocate up to $100 at their discretion. Anything more than $100 is taken to the membership.

Communal discernment remains at the heart of our decision making and, like the first Christians in the Book of Acts, we seek to be of one mind, one heart, and one accord. We do not vote yes or no on motions. Rather, proposals are introduced, discussed, and eventually decided upon. Proposals seldom remain as they were introduced but are improved or modified to meet people's concerns as necessary. When it is time to decide, people either give consent to the proposal, stand aside from it (abstain), or block it. We have only had two blocks in the history of Radical Living. Although communal discernment is not the most efficient decision-making process, it does effectively allow each person to have a voice. Sometimes it takes many months to make a final decision, particularly when it involves our Way or Praxis.

Conflict Resolution

An inside joke in our community is that Radical Living should be called Regular Living, since in many ways people have the same conflicts they would have in most living situations (who keeps leaving their socks in the bathroom, whose turn is it to clean the kitchen, and so on). The difference between other living situations is that the members of Radical Living have consciously chosen to share their lives with others in an intentional way. We share common values and recognize Christ as the one who strengthens and sustains us, heals and redeems us. Thus when conflict arises, we seek to address those issues.

When there is a conflict between members, we refer to Matthew 18:15–20 as our guide to resolve the issue at hand. The following is our *conflict resolution* protocol. All members agree to attempt to solve problems by first dealing directly with the person or persons with whom she is experiencing conflict. Implicit in this agreement is a commitment to state the matter in love, honestly and openly. If there is still no resolution, the members in conflict will ask a mutually agreed-upon member to help mediate and solve the problem with those having the conflict. If there is still no resolution, the members in conflict will formally request assistance from the community in solving the problem. The goal of conflict resolution is not to find who is right and who is wrong, but to restore relationship.

Leadership

In 2011, I was licensed as a pastor by the Mennonite Church, but in reality my wife and I co-pastor the community of Radical Living. Rather than the word "pastor," we use the term "community steward." In regard to our leadership model, we look to the Scriptures and also the Trinity. In community, we lean on one another's strengths and humbly acknowledge our weaknesses. As stated on the back cover of liberation theologian Leonardo Boff's *Holy Trinity, Perfect Community,* "the church, like the Trinity, is best expressed not as a hierarchy of power but as a community of diverse gifts and functions" (cf. John 17:21; Acts 2:44–45, 4:34–36). Other leadership roles include hospitality coordinator, treasurer, and membership coordinator. As a community, we have come to understand that leadership is a function and not a title. We have realized that we are all leaders in certain areas and we are followers in other areas, and that there needs to be a space for both. Yet, it is essential if our community is to thrive that we are committed to serving and loving one another, our neighbors, and to acknowledging that Christ is our head.

Ministries

Our ministries include hospitality, finance, prayer, neighborhood, and a food pantry we call loaves and fishes. Each ministry works as a committee, and the coordinators of each ministry meet together once a month to discuss ways to support one another. There are times when we must take issues from our organizational meeting to the membership meeting, yet the ministry and organizational meetings have allowed our membership meetings to serve as a deeper time of fellowship and sharing, and less about bureaucracy and organizational administration.

This is the current form of our community. It has changed significantly since it was founded, and it will continue to develop and take new shape as new members join and long-term members realize the need to remain dynamic.

Making a Rule

A rule can positively shape the life of an individual, family, and faith community. Developing a rhythm, identifying shared values, employing a model for conflict resolution, and commitment to pray for one another strengthens the prayer lives of all involved. By committing to share faith with one another we learn about each other's challenges, biases, joys, and disappointments. We get the opportunity to support, and occasionally correct, one another, and we enter into service with one another to accomplish tasks, realize dreams, and address injustices.

Several years ago a member of Radical Living sent an anti-immigrant e-mail to the membership. Most of the membership strongly believes that the biblical texts relating to hospitality for the stranger are applicable to the contemporary issue of immigration. Thus many members were frustrated with the e-mail and did not know how to respond to it. We employed our rhythm to deepen our understanding of immigration. We began a series of Bible studies that explored immigration and spent time praying for the issue. Several members decided to volunteer at an immigration clinic, and over the course of several months, our community was connected to various ways to serve immigrants in our neighborhood.

The person who sent the e-mail eventually softened her stance and helped to organize a symposium called "Theology of Immigration: God, Immigrant and Activism," which brought in speakers from across the country to explore immigration through a biblical lens. It was hosted by a local church, and the event raised money for several immigrant families whose head of household is awaiting deportation. The biggest step was our partnership with the New Sanctuary Movement, in which we housed Roxroy Salmon, an undocumented immigrant facing deportation. Roxroy moved to the United States from Jamaica when he was eighteen years old. As a young man he was arrested for marijuana possession but served no time. He married and had two children, a daughter now in college and a son now in middle school. Roxroy has been married for more than twenty years. At his mother's prompting he decided to apply for citizenship. Unfortunately, due to his one arrest, he was given an order of deportation. His son struggled deeply, acting out and struggling with his academic work, yet all the time staying as close as possible to his father for fear of losing him. Radical Living opened our hospitality room to him for three months in the hope that he would be able to find a way out of deportation. He eventually moved to another house provided by New Sanctuary Coalition, which is an interfaith network of congregations, organizations, and individuals who stand in solidarity with immigrants (and their families) who are facing deportation. Roxroy is still in the process of seeking residency. By that time the person who had sent the initial e-mail was our hospitality coordinator and was charged with the task of leading our hospitality efforts. Through prayer, Bible study, and fellowship, she was formed by the cloud of witnesses.

Spiritual disciplines are ways in which we participate in the Kingdom revolution that transforms the individual and society, and even in cosmic redemption (but that is another topic). It is through disciplines, such as prayer, fasting, and fellowship, that we have breakthroughs, experience deliverance, and work out our salvation.

Chapter 9

Destiny of Radical Disciples

Truly, I say to you, there will not be left here one stone upon another that will not be thrown down.

—Jesus

Generations do not cease to be born, and we are responsible to them because we are the only witnesses they have. The sea rises, the light fails, lovers cling to each other and children cling to us. The moment we cease to hold each other, the moment we break faith with one another, the sea engulfs us and the light goes out.

—James Baldwin, *The Fire Next Time*

Most participants in emerging, countercultural Christian movements, such as the Christian intentional community movement or the emerging church, are young, white evangelical or mainline Christians. They often come from middle-class rural or suburban backgrounds, and have little experience interacting with people of color or others from a different socioeconomic class, particularly within an urban context. These movements also have participation, although to a much lesser extent, by people of color and those who are marginalized in society (including the formerly homeless and undocumented immigrants). Many of the prominent speakers and authors are Euro-Americans with great capacity to self-promote, particularly in a context that privileges white males, and those who are equipped to navigate the world they have created.

Almost ten years into the intentional Christian community movement, the movement that I am most deeply connected to, the emphasis continues to be on the development of new intentional communities, while there remains scarce support or resources for the spiritual formation of those who are living in community. My question for these communities is twofold: (1) How does the church develop the young, white, and middle-class participants to grasp fully the theological implications of living in solidarity with the poor and marginalized? (2) How does the church encourage and develop among those deemed outcast by society an understanding of their importance and primary place in what Dr. King called the Beloved Community? The church must be engaged in seeking answers to these questions if she wants to remain faithful to proclaiming the Gospel.

If a new movement of intentional communities is to be sustainable, be prophetic, and have a deep impact on the neighborhoods, cities, and cultures in which they exist, it is important to support the spiritual formation of the members of these communities. There has been much effort to maintain the momentum of this movement, developing networks and launching more communities, yet there has been a significant lack of discipleship within these communities. An exception to this is the work of David Janzen and the Nurturing Communities Project. Janzen, a member of Reba Place Fellowship in Chicago, is an elder in the movement. Through the Nurturing Communities Project he has mentored many young communitarians, myself included. Yet he is only one person and thus has limited capacity.

Many of the young, white Christians who have moved from the suburbs to an urban context have not yet been fully radicalized (rooted in the prophetic Christian tradition) and still maintain vestiges of a colonizer mentality, which can damage relations with neighbors and also block their spiritual growth. By *colonizer mentality,* I mean that too often, young people come to the city with the internalized idea that they are saving the poor and people of color. If the church is to move toward a postcolonial perspective, it will have to acknowledge and address the unjust rhetoric, institutions, and biases that continue to pervade the church today.

Often those who confess Christ are the ones who perpetuate dangerous rhetoric that not only hinders, but destroys the prophetic message of the church. The church swings back and forth from the liberal to conservative perspective while rarely deepening in Christ and the promise of the coming Kingdom. Thus the church in the United States is becoming increasingly irrelevant. She is, in fact, not only in decline, but dying. Yet, there is hope in this movement of intentional communities who continue in the tradition of the "schools of prophets" (2 Kings 2:3, 2:5, 4:38). Like the ancient prophets, participants in this new movement are well positioned to be a voice within the church as well as a voice to the church. These communities have the opportunity to awaken a sleeping and often divided church, and to call to remembrance our calling: "to do justice, and to love kindness, and to walk humbly with your God" (Mic. 6:8).

Dr. King shifted from the language of Beloved Community to Kingdom of God during the latter years of his ministry. It is time for a prophetic shift to occur not only in various movements and submovements of Christianity, but in the church itself. We must repent of dogmas and ideologies, and return to Jesus' teachings, modeling our lives on his life. We must repent of *christianities* that promote bigotry, systemic injustices, and self-righteousness. The language of the Kingdom of God is prophetic; it implies regime change. It is political and assumes an eventual overturn of the current system. Whereas the notion of a Beloved Community points to the people, the Kingdom of God points to the King who reigns justly and restores peace and blessing. Community is important, and we must work toward equity and justice among our sisters and brothers throughout the world; and yet the language of Kingdom implies an entirely new order. And if we are not part of that order, we are part of the disorder of this world.

Most first-century Jews expected the Messiah to arrive in glory as a king who would restore the nation of Israel to a place of prominence. They were wrong. Many today paint Christ to be nothing more than a political revolutionary or, conversely, as a supporter of the status quo. Most Christians today are expecting the Messiah to return in much the same manner as expected by first-century Jews. Christians expect Christ to return with fire in his eyes, sword in hand, descending from the heavens on a white horse, ready to crush violently all who oppose him. Are we able to open our minds and allow our imaginations to be stirred by the Holy Spirit in a way that allows the light and love of Christ to shine into our lives and into the lives of those around us in a way that might surprise us?

What if Jesus does not return with a sword in his hand, fire in his eyes, and riding on a cloud? When the Messiah walked the earth two thousand years ago, the people for the most part did not believe Jesus was the promised Messiah because they were expecting that militant Messiah who would flex his muscles and crush his enemies. What if Christ's second coming is similarly sublime? John, Peter, and Paul say (Rev. 16:15; 2 Pet. 3:10; 1 Thess. 5:2) that the day of the Lord will come *like a thief in the night*. Like a thief, Christ may return quietly. Those who have wealth and power may awaken one day to discover they have been stripped of their power and prestige—their inner poverty revealed.

The Scriptures say that the Kingdom of God is near, it is at hand, and it is within each of us. Jesus compares the good news to a seed. The Kingdom of God is like a flower opening. It takes incredible patience to watch a flower open. Most will never watch the entire process from closed bud to full bloom. What if one day we look and see the fullness of the Kingdom manifest all around and within us, with Christ the King sitting on his holy throne—the flower in full bloom, never to wilt? It is important to prepare for Christ's return in whatever form it manifests. We must watch and yearn for his return, but we must also do the work of preparing the world for him.

Preparing the Kindling

In what way will God's Kingdom enter in? And how will the coming Kingdom overturn the wicked system? In the Hebrew Scriptures, God re-created the world with the flood and set the rainbow in the sky as a promise not to flood the world again. But that does not mean God's destruction will never again rain down on this world. In Peter's second letter, he prophesied fire next time (2 Pet. 3:7). The fire will bring about the renewal and redemption of the world and creation. Just as repentance is twofold (both turning from sin and toward God), so God's fire is also twofold. The fire is destructive, but it is also regenerative.

The only way we can live the way God wants us to is by the power of Spirit. John the Baptizer said about Jesus, "I baptize you with water for repentance, but one who is more powerful than I is coming after me; I am not worthy to carry his sandals. He will baptize you with the Holy Spirit and fire" (Matt. 3:11). Fire penetrates to the inner most being, it consumes quickly, it destroys and ignites. It comes like a prairie fire burning old growth so that new life may grow.

This God of fire pervades the Holy Scriptures. The author of the Letter to the Hebrews wrote, "Our God is a consuming fire" (Heb. 12:29). Jesus said, "I have come to bring fire on earth, and how I wish it were already kindled" (Luke 12:49). In the Book of Daniel, Shadrach, Meshach, and Abednego went into the fiery furnace and were not burned. In fact, a fourth person—the living God—was in the furnace with them. The blessing is that God does not leave us alone in the fire—neither does God leave us in the fire. The time in the fire produces holiness and intimacy with God. This fire is necessary. It burns up sin and iniquity, and separates the wheat from the chaff. It is used to consecrate us, purify us, and make us holy. It brings conviction upon the sinner and sanctifies the saint.

Malachi wrote, "When he comes, he is a purifier of silver" (Mal. 3:3). God is the refiner, and we are in the furnace. God heats it and stokes it and the fire blazes hotter, and it burns up our pride, lust, temper, and unforgiveness. Our sin and iniquity are burned up. We are refined and purified until the refiner, the one who breathed us into being, can look and see his reflection within us. God wants to reflect his beauty in our life.

The church has lost her fire. And too often unconsecrated fire, like that offered by Nadab and Abihu, is offered; this unconsecrated fire has no power to transform lives, but merely offers false hope and creates an emotional frenzy, while neglecting the poor and oppressed, marginalized, and disenfranchised. The church needs Spirit to be alive and active in this world for God's glory.

The fire on the altar must continue to flame through worship, prayer, the study of Holy Scripture, and fellowship. Samuel Chadwick, the twentieth-century Methodist pastor, wrote, "A fireless altar is the sign of desertion and death. It means the temple has lost its God." We must pray for more fire. God says, "So, because you are lukewarm, and neither hot nor cold, I will spit you out of my mouth" (Rev. 3:16). God cannot stand a lukewarm heart. When our heart yearns for God, the Spirit manifests in our lives. "Then I will be found of you when you seek me with all your heart" (Jer. 29:13).

Encountering the Spirit

There are no references in Scripture of Jesus baptizing anyone in water. Rather, Jesus introduces us to the person of the Spirit. Scripture proves that water baptism and fire baptism are both ordained by God. The disciples of Jesus were not changed merely by his teachings. It took fire baptism to transform them. Anthropologists say when humanity discovered fire, our lives changed drastically. This is true today. When a person discovers the fire of the Holy Spirit, their life is transformed. It is by the atoning blood of Jesus Christ that we are saved, and it is by the Spirit that we are given power.

As the Father and Son are persons, so the Spirit is also a person. If we want to learn about a person, we must study what they are about, where they are from, what they have done, and what they are able to do; but if we want to know a person, we must do more than study, we must experience and spend time in that person's presence.

In the Scriptures, we learn that the Holy Spirit is a holy fire; a creative, life-giving force and a rushing mighty wind; the Comforter and Christ's gift; the Spirit is the Oil of Gladness; the third person of the Trinity and the breath of Jesus; the Holy Spirit is the Spirit of the Living God, the Spirit of Jesus that dwells within each of us who seek and receive the Spirit.

The Spirit has incredible purpose in the life of every Christian believer. Spirit reveals Christ to us and through us to others, gives power to the believer, teaches us to pray, and even prays for us. Spirit searches our heart and convicts us of sin, and brings to our attention Scripture and its meaning in time of need. Spirit is the Master of the house, which is our body as well as the body of believers gathered to meet God. Spirit baptizes the believer and gives us faithfulness to serve and boldness to testify to the work that God has done in our lives. Spirit fills us with the fullness of God and anoints us for service.

Spirit Power

When Christ, who is pure and holy, was baptized in the River Jordan, the Holy Spirit descended upon him in the form of a dove. But because we are sinful, the Holy Spirit must come to us as a blazing fire so that we might be made holy. It is the fire of the Holy Spirit that convicts us of sin. It is the fire that brings to light the darkness. And it is the fire that burns out the impurities of sin and beckons us toward holiness.

We must allow the fire to continue its work in us. We must preach and teach with fire, pray with fire and worship with fire. There must be enthusiasm for Spirit in fellowship. For fifty days after Christ ascended to the right hand of the Father, there were no conversions. Then during Pentecost, which is the Jewish feast of harvest, the fire came, and three thousand people were transformed into believers. That is the power of the Holy Spirit fire.

We must be like the bush that blazed but was not consumed; Shadrach, Meshach, and Abednego who went into the furnace but were not burned; gold and silver whose quality improves by prolonged contact with fire. We must blaze but not be burned. Be fireproof. Be like the deep things of God that are made closer to God by the fire.

Paul wrote in his first letter to the church in Corinth that God has "put his Spirit in our hearts as a deposit." I interpret this to mean that Spirit-filled people live from the heart. Salvation is more than mental affirmation of proper doctrine. It is seeking God in earnestness and humility. The church needs to pray that God sends a generation of saints and prophets who are more concerned with the church's holiness than its happiness. We need a generation who will reclaim the victory and set this world on fire for God.

Reclaiming a Right Fear of God

Most believers have lost their fear of God. They may fear the government, or media, or their boss, or that they do not have the right clothes or enough education, or some other thing. Too often we associate *fear* with abuse. Yet fear also implies reverence and awe. God is the highest authority and is the one who set all things into order and being. Thus we must have a healthy awe, reverence, and fear of God. When we do not fear God, we fear the things of this world. Fear, rightly placed, produces holy boldness and deep faith. It strengthens us to speak out and act against the things that God hates, such as exploitation of the poor, systematic oppression, and bigotry. We must fear God in a way that frees us from the yoke that the world attempts to place upon us and strengthens us for the work of building God's Kingdom *on earth as it is in heaven*. When we are filled with the Spirit of the Lord, revere the Holy One, and share life in a community of sisters and brothers who challenge, encourage, and equip us to deepen and mature as saints, our glimpses of the Kingdom of God gradually expand to a holy vision of God's promise for a new creation.